MAN ABOUT THE KITCHEN

MAN ABOUT THE KITCHEN

Recipes for the Reluctant Chef

ALASTAIR WILLIAMS

summersdale

Summersdale Publishers Ltd
46 West Street
Chichester
West Sussex
PO19 1RP
UK

www.summersdale.com

Printed and bound in Great Britain

CONTENTS

Start Here ...

There are an awful lot of men out there who are struggling to get through the burger and baked bean barrier. Fear not, help is at hand. Although this book will not turn you into the next 'super chef', it will teach you how to cook a variety of dishes ranging from simple stir-fries to mouthwatering cakes.

Cooking is regarded by many as a chore, its purpose being purely to sustain life with as little effort as possible. Perhaps you rarely cook for yourself, preferring to rely on takeaways or ready-to-eat meals. If you are one such person then it's time to change. Being able to cook is not solely a useful social skill; it should provide enjoyment and entertainment. Not only is it nice to cook for a partner, but it is also something that can be enjoyed together. Another benefit from being able to cook is that it might get you out of the washing-up if you have prepared the meal.

Cooking combines creativity, skill, timing and knowledge, plus at the end of it you can eat what you have created, which is one up on an oil painting! You might not give a stuff about how the meal looks provided it tastes good and there is plenty of it; each to their own. The intent of this book is simply to get you cooking as quickly and easily as possible.

The Rudiments

Being a good cook does not mean that you have to be able to create dazzling masterpieces every time you enter a kitchen. Learning how to cook is a gradual process that takes time and patience. Even the most experienced chefs have disasters. Remember that cooking is an art, not a science. You will find that even when you follow a recipe word for word it does not always turn out the way it should. If you repeat a recipe several times over it is unlikely that it will ever taste or look exactly the same. With experience you will learn how to adapt recipes to your own tastes and skills.

One of the best ways of improving your cooking is to watch other cooks. This is where you pick up the little tricks and secrets that will enable you to increase your knowledge and skill. It is sensible to keep a small notebook so that you can jot down ideas and tips that you come across. Half the fun of cooking is in experimenting, using old skills and recipes and combining them with new ideas.

Kitchen Equipment

Any craftsman will have a set of tools that is essential to his trade. The same principle applies to the cook. There is a plethora of gadgets and gizmos on the market for cooks. It is very easy to believe that they are all essential; it is only when you see your cupboards bursting with juicers, toasted sandwich-makers, blenders, steamers, and yogurt-makers that you realise you have little room left for the food. Although some gadgets can aid the chef, speeding up laborious tasks such as grating cheese, others are dispensable and will soon find their way to the back of the cupboard after the novelty has worn off. As a rule, it is far better to buy a few quality items than a number of inferior products. A frying pan that bends under the weight of a couple of sausages is going to be useless. Quality in cooking equipment often equates to weight; a pan should have a thick bottom and a sturdy handle. However, a saucepan that is so heavy that you need to start body-building before you can pick it up is not necessarily going to be the best one for you.

Kitchen Knives

Investing in a quality set of knives is essential. Very few people have adequate kitchen knives, often relying on blunt, flimsy instruments that are potentially dangerous. When choosing knives, bear in mind the job for which they are intended; it is difficult to use a 10-inch blade to peel fruit. I generally use just two sizes, a small cook's knife with a 3-inch blade, and a large 7-inch knife. It is also useful to have a serrated knife for cutting fruit. If you have the choice between buying a cheap set of knives and a couple of high-quality knives, go for the latter.

The Freezer

The main advantage of having a freezer is that large quantities of food can be stored and used as and when required. If you arrive home late and are feeling too tired to cook it is a joy to be able to go to the freezer and take out a ready-prepared meal. They can also save you time and money as food can be bought and prepared in bulk. When cooking a pasta sauce why not make double the amount and freeze what is unused? A freezer is also useful for storing seasonal fruit and vegetables, so you can enjoy them any time of year.

To aid fast freezing, do not place large quantities of unfrozen food into the freezer at one go. This raises the temperature of the freezer and slows down the freezing process. Food that has been cooked should always be cold before being placed in the freezer.

If you are low on food or have an unexpected guest then there should ideally be something in the freezer that you can use. This is where the problem begins: do you know what is in your freezer and, perhaps more importantly, how long it has been there? It amazes me how many people's freezer contents lack any type of labelling. If your freezer is organised you will save both time and money.

• Label and date all the items in your freezer. It is also a good idea to keep a separate list on the outside of the freezer door that you can update every time you add or remove something from the freezer.

• Freezers run more efficiently when they are full, so try to keep your freezer well stocked, even if it is half full of bread.

• If you want to make full use of your freezer, then it is worth investing in a book that provides information on the different methods of preparing food for the freezer, as well as telling you what can be frozen and for how long. Don't think that just because it is frozen you can retrieve a steak and kidney pie that your mother made for you in 1979.

Common Sense and the Kitchen

Cooking requires a degree of common sense. The recipes in this book are created with simplicity in mind, both in terms of implements and cooking skills required. However, I don't want to be held responsible for a person who ends up in Casualty for having misunderstood the instruction 'stand in boiling water for 20 minutes'.

Another important point to remember is that all cooking times and temperatures are approximate. Not all ovens will take the same length of time to cook a meal. If, for example, your oven is fan assisted, you will have to allow for the extra efficiency. Cooking is ultimately intuitive and no number of instructions can replace this. Before you try any recipe read through it first to make sure you have the ingredients and the time to prepare it.

The Kitchen

Just as a well-organised garage has a wide selection of high-quality tools and adequate working space, the same applies to the kitchen. The purpose of a kitchen is to prepare food, therefore the element of hygiene must not be ignored. If you are a bachelor, then it is perfectly understandable to want to show your independence by being as messy as possible. However, once you reach the stage of the overflowing bin surrounded by empty takeaway boxes you know it is time to consider clearing up.

The three main areas to consider are organisation, safety, and hygiene.

Organisation and Safety

• Keep heavy items in the lower cupboards.

• Never use a stool to stand on whilst trying to reach an object. Even a chair can be unstable, so ideally you should have a small kitchen step-ladder.

• The kitchen should be well ventilated so fumes and heat are removed quickly.

• There should be plenty of light, natural or artificial.

• A fire blanket and extinguisher should be kept handy.

• Keep cupboards tidy.

• Take care with the positioning of pans on your cooker, and remember to keep the handles from protruding over the edge.

• Make sure that handles on pots and pans are not loose.

• Keep an eye out for damaged flexes on electrical appliances such as toasters and kettles.

• Use caution when using electrical gadgets such as blenders and food processors.

• Keep matches and sharp knives out of reach of children.

• Knives should be kept sharp, as a blunt knife can slip when cutting and cause an accident.

• Kitchen knives should be kept in a knife block. Keeping them in a drawer not only causes the knives to lose their sharpness, but also makes it easy to cut oneself.

Fat Fires

If a pan of fat ignites, remain calm and follow these rules:

• Never throw water on top of the oil – this will make it worse.

• Turn off the gas or electric hob if you can safely do so, otherwise wait until the fire has been extinguished.

• The most effective way to put out a fat fire is to get a dampened tea towel and place it over the top of the pan. Do not remove it for at least five minutes after the flames have subsided.

• If the fire is out of control, call the fire brigade and leave the house.

Hygiene

Not wishing to get into the gory details, being violently sick is often a consequence of bad hygiene. Harmful bacteria can spread quickly in the right conditions, so here are a few guidelines.

• All surfaces such as worktops, floors and cookers should be cleaned regularly, preferably every day.

• Never let your kitchen surfaces get cluttered. Clean up as you go along. This makes food preparation easier, as well as reducing the burden of cleaning at the end.

• Clean the door seals on fridges and freezers on a regular basis.

• Keep cooking utensils clean.

• Don't leave meat or fish out of the fridge for any lengthy period, especially if it has been cooked.

• Throw away food that passed its 'use by' date.

• Wash all fruit and vegetables.

• Make sure meat is sufficiently cooked. If you like your meat rare, it must be as fresh as possible.

• Allow large pieces of frozen meat to defrost completely before cooking.

You Want Me To What? A Glossary of Cooking Terms

Although some cooking terms might seem obvious there are probably many of you out there who will have trouble even finding the kitchen, let alone understanding recipe instructions.

Baste
To spoon fat or oil over food in order to keep it moist. Usually done to a joint of meat intermittently during roasting.

Beat
This is the mixing of ingredients using a wooden spoon, a fork or a whisk.

Chop
To cut into small pieces.

Cream
To mix fat with another ingredient such as sugar until it becomes creamy.

Dice
To cut into small cubes.

Grate
A grater can produce coarse or fine shavings of food, such as cheese or vegetables.

Knead
To use your knuckles to smooth dough out, the idea being to create a smooth texture.

Marinade
A combination of juices, spices or oils in which meat is soaked to enhance the flavour.

Parboil
This is the partial boiling of something. The cooking will then normally be completed by another method. This applies, for example, to roast potatoes.

Peel
To remove the skin or outer layer of a vegetable or fruit.

Rub in
To rub flour and fat together between your fingertips until it resembles breadcrumbs.

Simmer
To cook just below boiling point so that only an occasional bubble appears on the surface.

Weights and Measures

There are certain things that indicate our age – comments such as 'during the war' and 'I remember when you got a couple of lamb chops for a shilling'. You might be asking what a couple of lamb chops and 'the War' have to do with food. Well, not a lot, but somewhere in the mists of time the country went Metric. Those Imperial days are now long gone, but many people still prefer to think in Imperial weights and measures, as I do myself. Hence the need to be able to convert Metric to Imperial and vice versa. Other amounts are referred to in spoons or cups, which are self-explanatory.

The following abbreviations are used:

tbsp = tablespoon   tsp = teaspoon

If you don't possess a set of kitchen scales then it is possible to convert certain ingredients into spoon measures. All spoon measures refer to level spoons, not heaped. Obviously the weights of all ingredients will vary, but here are some rough measures:

1 tbsp = 1 oz (25 g) of ... syrup, jam, honey
2 tbsp = 1 oz (25 g) of ... butter, margarine, lard, sugar
3 tbsp = 1 oz (25 g) of ... cornflour, cocoa, flour
4 tbsp = 1 oz (25 g) of ... grated cheese, porridge oats

1 tsp = 5 ml
1 tbsp = 15 ml
1 mug of rice weighs roughly 8 oz (225 g)

The approximations used for conversion between Metric and Imperial in this book are as follows:

1 oz = 25 g	2 oz = 50 g
3 oz = 75 g	4 oz = 100 g
6 oz = 150 g	8 oz = 225 g
1 lb = 500 g	

¼ pint = 150 ml	½ pint = 300 ml
1 pint = 600 ml	2 pints = 1 litre

Gas Mark	Celsius	Fahrenheit
1	140 °	275 °
2	150 °	300 °
3	170 °	325 °
4	180 °	350 °
5	200 °	400 °
6	225 °	425 °
7	230 °	450 °
8	240 °	475 °
9	250 °	500 °

Healthy Eating

Healthy eating is something that many of us give little thought to – decadence is more fun, after all. But if your idea of a balanced diet means equal amounts of food to alcohol, you should read this section.

As the old saying goes, 'We are what we eat': if you eat a lot of lard you tend to look like it. Aesthetics aside, heart disease, high blood pressure and numerous other illnesses are linked to poor eating habits.

If you want to stay healthy you must have a balanced diet. Try to:

- Eat at least five portions of fruit and vegetables (not including potatoes) a day.

- Reduce the amount of fat you eat, and replace saturated fats (for example, butter, lard, and suet) with polyunsaturated and monounsaturated fats (for example, olive oil and margarine).

- Reduce the amount of salt you eat.

- Try to eat oily fish (for example, fresh tuna, salmon, trout, mackerel, and sardines) at least twice a week.

- Eat plenty of carbohydrates (bread, pasta, rice, cereals and potatoes).

- Try to stick to 1–2 units of alcohol a day.

Store Cupboard Essentials

A well-stocked store cupboard is essential for any cook. Although a degree of improvisation is possible there are a number of basic ingredients that you should always keep in stock. It is a common problem when cooking that whatever ingredients you have in your cupboard will always be the things you don't need, while whatever you do need will be conspicuous by its absence. Some suggestions for your pantry are:

- flour (plain and self-raising)
- cornflour
- yeast
- salt
- sugar

- rice (short and long grain)
- pasta (various kinds)
- noodles
- couscous

- chilli powder
- curry powder
- cumin
- coriander
- turmeric
- oregano

- rosemary
- paprika
- black peppercorns
- thyme
- cinnamon
- cloves
- ground ginger
- nutmeg
- all spice

- stock cubes (various kinds)
- honey
- vanilla essence
- lemon juice
- mayonnaise
- soy sauce
- sun-dried tomatoes
- Worcestershire sauce
- tomato paste
- tomato sauce
- chilli sauce
- curry paste
- vinegar (white and balsamic)
- extra-virgin olive oil (for salads)
- vegetable/sunflower oil (for cooking)
- walnut oil (for salads and baking)
- sesame oil (for Oriental dishes)

- tinned tomatoes
- tinned kidney beans
- tinned tuna
- tinned fruit (various kinds)

STORE CUPBOARD ESSENTIALS

- olives
- anchovies
- lemons
- onions
- potatoes
- garlic

- butter
- eggs
- cheese (various kinds)

Choosing Meat, Poultry and Fish

Although there are many tantalising and of course healthy vegetarian meals, the allure of meat is too strong to ignore. A fillet steak cooked to perfection with a green salad and french fries is absolutely delicious.

Beef

When choosing a piece of beef it should be a light red colour and slightly elastic, without too much gristle. Avoid old beef, which appears dark in colour and the fat is often yellowish. There are many different cuts of beef, and each is suitable for different methods of cooking:

Roasting
topside, sirloin, fillet, ribs, rump

Grilling or Frying
sirloin, fillet, rump, entrecote, mince

Stewing
rump, brisket, flank, chuck

Pork

Pork is cheaper than beef and should be a pale pink colour, smooth on the surface and firm. In order to reduce the risk of food poisoning, ensure that the pork is cooked through.

Roasting
ribs, loin, leg, blade

Grilling or Frying
chops, ribs, loin

Lamb

Lamb should be a pinkish red colour, and the bones at the joints should be red.

Roasting
shoulder, leg, best end of neck, loin

Grilling or Frying
loin chops or cutlets, liver

Stewing
loin, leg, breast, liver

Chicken

Chicken is one of the cheapest of available meats as a result of factory breeding, however, there has been a sacrifice in flavour in favour of price. If you want to know how a chicken should taste, buy a free-range chicken. When buying chicken it should smell fresh and the flesh should be firm. Chicken is very versatile: most parts can be fried, roasted or stewed.

Fish

Most fish are caught commercially, and unless you fish for yourself or have friends who do so you are unlikely to be able to obtain locally caught fish. If you are lucky and live near the coast you may be able to buy freshly caught fish and shellfish directly from the fishermen.

If a recipe uses a whole fish it will need cleaning. The head, gills and innards have to be removed. Normally fish come already cleaned, but, if they don't, ask the fishmonger to do it for you.

When choosing fish, pick one that doesn't smell. The eyes should be bright and full. If the fish is not fresh the eyes will be dull. The gills should be slime-free, clean and shiny. If you press a fresh fish with your finger, the flesh should spring back up.

Fresh fish should be eaten on the day of purchase. Fish can be baked, poached, fried and grilled.

Carving Meat

There is definitely an art to carving, and it does take time to become a proficient carver. The most important thing about carving is having a sharp knife. It is very difficult to cut thin slices with a blunt knife. Get into the habit of sharpening the knife before use.

When cutting meat, cut across the grain; this makes it easier to chew, which is important if the meat is on the tough side. The meat should be cut with a gentle sawing action so that straight, whole slices are cut.

Usually when carving roast meat, juice from the meat gathers at the bottom of the carving plate. Use these juices when making gravy. When carving a leg of lamb, cut the meat parallel to the bone.

Preparing and Cooking Vegetables

Many people seem to have an aversion to anything that is healthy or fresh. Nutritionists are right when they say that we should increase the proportion of vegetables in our diets. In the past the supply of vegetables was determined by what was available locally according to season, but supermarkets now have exotic vegetables alongside local produce all year round. Although many of these imports are not cheap they do add tremendous variety.

There is still a tendency for people to overcook vegetables. Remember to time vegetables as they cook rather than leaving them indefinitely. Vegetables taste and look better when cooked correctly, and they retain more of their nutritional value.

Artichokes (Globe)

They are interesting vegetables in terms of shape and texture. When you buy artichokes, make sure they look and feel fresh with no brown tinges to the leaves.

Before cooking remove a few of the tough outer leaves, cut off the stalks, and then wash. Place in a pan of salted boiling water, reduce the heat to a simmer and continue to simmer until an outside leaf can be removed with ease. This should take about 30 minutes, depending on the size and age of the artichoke.

Drain well and serve. Remove the tough outer leaves to expose the tender ones. Dip in melted butter, then eat the fleshy part of the leaf, discarding the rest. The treasured piece of the artichoke is the heart, which is found at the bottom of the leaves. Do not eat the fluffy centre as it has an unpleasant taste.

As an alternative, serve the artichokes cold with a French dressing.

Asparagus

This is not your everyday vegetable, but it is well worth splashing out on once in a while. Try to use asparagus as soon as they are bought, don't keep it for days. When buying asparagus pick bundles that contain heads of the same size.

Untie the bundles and remove one to two inches off the stalk. Using a small knife, scrape downwards to remove the tough outer layer. Wash and tie back into bundles. Place the asparagus in a deep pan and simmer for about 10 minutes or until tender. Serve straight away with either butter, mayonnaise or Hollandaise sauce.

Aubergine/Eggplant

There are a number of varieties, but the most common are purple in colour. When buying aubergine choose those with a firm skin. Cut the top and bottom off, and then slice thinly. Before cooking extract the bitter juice that is present by sprinkling the slices lightly with salt and leaving for 20 minutes. Before cooking, rinse the slices in water, then pat dry with a paper towel. The usual method for cooking aubergines is to fry them either in oil or butter until they soften.

Baby Sweetcorn

This expensive import from the Orient is worth the price. The only preparation needed is washing (don't forget behind your ears), following which they can be gently boiled or fried. To benefit from their full flavour they need to retain their crispness, so don't overcook.

Beans – French

Wash, top and tail them. Cut into 1-inch lengths or leave whole. To cook, place in boiling salted water and cook for 10 to 15 minutes. After cooking they can be tossed in butter.

Broccoli

Wash in cold water. Cut off the stalks then divide into flowerets (clumps). Place in boiling water for about 10 minutes. Don't overcook as the broccoli will become mushy, losing most of its flavour and colour.

Brussels Sprouts

If there was one vegetable that was always overcooked at school it was the sprout. In those halcyon days you weren't allowed to leave the table until you had cleared your plate.

Remove the outer leaves and cut off the stalk. It should not be removed entirely, otherwise all the leaves will fall off. Cut a cross in the base and then wash in cold water. Boil in water with a pinch of salt for 10 minutes.

Cabbage

Remove the tough outer leaves and the centre stalk. You can either shred or quarter the leaves. To cook the shredded cabbage, place in boiling water for about 5 minutes. If the leaves are bigger they will need about 10 minutes.

Carrots

Top and tail the carrots and then peel. Before cooking they can be quartered or sliced. Baby carrots can be cooked whole. Boil in salted water for 15 to 20 minutes. Carrots can be eaten raw in salads or roasted in oil when cooking a roast dinner.

Cauliflower

Wash in cold water and then divide into flowerets. Boil in salted water until tender – about 10 minutes, depending on the size of the flowerets. Cauliflower can also be eaten raw and used as a crudité.

Courgettes

Having been force-fed these for years, I have almost come to like them. First of all, give them a wash, then top and tail them. Slice thinly and fry in butter or oil for about 10 minutes.

Garlic

When choosing garlic look for firm undamaged bulbs. Should you see any sign of green shoots appearing from the top of the bulb, don't buy it. Garlic that is past its best will dry out and be unusable.

Garlic should be stored in a dry place. Special terracotta garlic pots are good if you are only keeping small quantities.

Garlic can give a subtle addition to a salad by rubbing the inside of a salad bowl with a cut clove. When garlic is uncooked and used raw it is in its most powerful state; cooking garlic reduces its potency. Garlic can be sliced, chopped, or crushed according to the flavour required. Slicing gives the most mild effect, then chopping and finally crushing.

Leeks

Remove the dark green section of the stalk and wash. They can either be sliced into rings, quartered or even left whole. To cook either boil for 10 to 15 minutes, or fry in oil or butter for about 10 minutes.

Mangetout

If you haven't seen these before, they look like pea pods that have been squashed by a lorry, but they taste delicious and are arguably worth the extortionate amount you will be charged for them.

To prepare your mangetout, wash, top and tail. If boiling, they need only 3 or 4 minutes because they maintain their flavour better when still crisp. They can also be fried gently in butter for a few minutes until they soften slightly. They make a colourful addition to stir-fries.

Mushrooms

The many types of mushroom available range from the standard button variety to the more exotic oyster or shitake. Some mushrooms can be eaten raw, but always clean them first.

Wipe the mushrooms with a damp cloth. Either remove or trim the stalk and then slice or leave whole. The mushrooms can be fried or grilled. To fry, melt a little oil or butter in a frying pan and cook for 3 to 4 minutes, depending on size. To grill, put under a hot grill with a light covering of butter. Mushrooms can be a great addition to many sauces.

Onions

The best way to stop your eyes watering when chopping onions is to get someone else to do it!

Top and tail the onion first, then peel off the outer layer. It can be chopped vertically or sliced into rings. Onions are normally fried in oil for about 5 minutes. They can be boiled in salted water for about 10 minutes. When frying onions take care that you don't burn them as this can taint a whole meal, even if only a few of the onions are burnt.

Parsnips

Top and tail, then peel and chop into largish pieces or thick slices. Parsnips can be boiled, fried or roasted.

Place in boiling water with a pinch of salt for about 20 minutes or until they are tender. If they are to be fried they need to be cut into thin slices or chips, otherwise they will not cook all the way through. Perhaps the nicest way of cooking parsnips is to bake them. Place the parsnips in an ovenproof dish with a couple of tablespoons of oil, and bake in a hot oven for about 40 minutes. They can be basted like roast potatoes.

Peas

If you have fresh peas (still in the pod), shell them and wash in cold water. To cook the peas, place them in boiling water for about 10 minutes.

Peppers

Available in red, green, yellow and orange. They all have different flavours – the lighter in colour they are, the sweeter they are, so the yellow ones are the sweetest and the green ones the most bitter.

Top and tail, then remove the core and seeds. Slice into rings, then halve and fry in a little oil for 5 minutes or so.

They can also be eaten raw and are particularly tasty in salads. Try the stuffed pepper recipe in this book as a third alternative.

Potatoes

Just as the Italians have their pasta, we seem to be mad about potatoes. We serve them in various guises, be it chips, crisps, roasted, boiled or mashed.

There are two basic types of potato: 'new' and 'old'. Both are now available all year round, although new potatoes are cheaper in the summer. Allow one or two potatoes per person, depending on your appetite and the size of the potato.

All potatoes need to be peeled or scrubbed before cooking.

Boiled

After peeling or scrubbing the potato, cut into halves or quarters, depending on its size, then place in salted boiling water for 15 to 20 minutes or until tender all the way through.

Mashed

If you want mashed potato make sure they are well cooked: you should be able to pass a knife through them easily. If they are not well cooked the mashed potatoes will have lumps in, however hard you try to remove them. Drain the potatoes, add a knob of butter and a drop of milk, then, using a potato masher, squash until they are nice and creamy, adding more milk and black pepper if required.

Roast

There are a number of ways to produce roast potatoes. Obviously having a potato and an oven is a good starting point. Peel the potatoes, then halve or quarter them depending on their size. Parboil for 5 minutes in salted boiling water. Drain the potatoes in a colander and shake so that the surface of the potatoes are slightly flaky (this produces crisp edges). Place the semi-cooked potatoes on a baking tray with some oil and place in the oven on Gas Mark 6 (220 °C, 425 °F) near the top of the oven if possible. Baste the potatoes with the oil a couple times while they are cooking. Roast the potatoes until they are golden and verging on crispiness, between 60 and 90 minutes.

Chips

These are a British institution, and they should of course be served with fish and wrapped in an old newspaper with lashings of vinegar and salt. If that description hasn't quelled your craving for chips then here is how to make your own.

Peel some old potatoes and cut into chip shapes. If you are feeling sophisticated slice them more thinly into french fries. The next stage is potentially dangerous, so take care. The chips need to be covered (at least partially) in oil to cook, so a large amount of oil is needed.

Heat the oil in a large frying pan. To test if the oil is hot enough, drop one chip in – if the oil bubbles loudly all around the chip it is up to temperature. Carefully add the chips, taking care not to throw them in the pan otherwise you may be splashed with hot oil. Fry the chips until they are crisp, making sure that the oil does not get too hot or start to smoke. Remember to turn the heat off as soon as you have finished frying.

Pumpkin

If you have a whole pumpkin, cut it into quarters, then remove all the seeds and pulp from the inside. Remove the skin and cut into chunks. To boil, place in salted boiling water for about 30 minutes. After the pumpkin has been boiled it can be fried in butter for 5 minutes.

Spinach

When buying spinach, buy more than you would if it was cabbage, for spinach will shrink considerably during cooking. Discard any yellowed leaves, then place in a small amount of boiling water for about 10 minutes. Grated nutmeg and spinach taste good together.

Swede

Peel and chop into chunks, then wash in cold water. Cook in salted boiling water for 20 to 25 minutes or until tender. Can be mashed with a knob of butter and black pepper.

Sweetcorn

Remove the husks and the ends, then place in boiling water for 10 minutes. Drain, then serve with butter and fresh black pepper.

Tomatoes

Fresh tomatoes can be fried in butter, grilled or baked. To remove the skin of a tomato, which should be done when making sauces, place in boiling water for about a minute. Remove from the hot water and cool them in cold water. The skins should now come away with ease.

Turnips

Peel and cut into chunks, then place in boiling water for 20 to 25 minutes or until tender.

How to Cook Pasta and Rice

Pasta is the basis of many Italian dishes, and its popularity has spread all over the world. Fresh pasta is worth buying if you are cooking for a special occasion as it tastes wonderful, or alternatively buy a pasta machine and make your own fresh pasta.

Pasta is normally served with a sauce, and here the imagination can really run wild. Once you have mastered some of the foundation sauces, such as a basic tomato sauce, you can go on to create your own. When producing sauces they should be reduced in volume to increase the intensity of the flavour. Do not boil rapidly but simmer gently. When you start to create your own recipes you will find that you gain even more satisfaction from cooking.

Cooking Pasta

Allow roughly 2–3 oz (50–75 g) of pasta per person.

Cooking pasta correctly is essential. Bring a large pan of water to the boil, then add a good pinch of salt. Add the pasta to the pan. Long pasta such as spaghetti should be eased gently into the pan, making sure that it is not broken. Adding a few of drops of olive oil can prevent the pasta from sticking together. The pasta should be cooked with the lid off, and stirred occasionally.

Normally, dried pasta requires 8 to 10 minutes in boiling water. While it should have some 'bite' to it (al dente), make sure that the pasta is not undercooked, as this could result in indigestion.

If you are cooking fresh pasta it normally only requires 2 or 3 minutes, so watch it carefully. There is a fine line with fresh pasta, with one minute it being perfect, then the next it is overcooked. Don't always go by the recommended time, taste the pasta whilst it is cooking. If you overcook your pasta it will stick together and taste very doughy.

Cooking Rice

There are two basic types of rice: long grain like basmati, which is fluffy and light when cooked, perfect for curries and stir-fries, and short grain, which sticks together and is used for things like sushi and rice pudding. In addition to white rice, you can also buy wild and brown varieties, which have a nuttier taste and a chewier texture.

Many people prefer to rinse the rice before cooking to get rid of excess rice dust, but it is not strictly necessary to do so. One cup of uncooked rice will make about three cups of cooked rice. Please note that the cooking times and water quantities vary slightly with different kinds of rice, and brown rice in particular takes longer to cook than white rice.

Boiling

Add the rice to cold, salted water, allowing approximately 2 cups of water for each cup of rice. Bring to the boil, then cover the pan and reduce the heat. Let it simmer until most of the liquid has been absorbed, then remove from the heat and leave to absorb the rest of the water. Don't lift the lid at this point, or it won't cook properly.

Microwave

Put the rice, water and salt into a microwave-safe dish, allowing 2 cups of water for each cup of rice. Cover, and microwave on high for five minutes, then on medium for 15 minutes.

Spices, Herbs and Seasonings

Cooking without herbs and spices is like looking at the world in black and white. There is something missing, a certain blandness. Used moderately, spices, herbs and seasonings can transform a plain meal into something special. Spices from around the world are available in most supermarkets, so it is possible to recreate authentic cuisine from as far afield as Thailand and the Caribbean. Just remember that the amounts used have to be carefully controlled, the idea being to enhance the flavour of the food, not to annihilate your taste buds. Many spices are available in different strengths such as chilli and curry powder, and there is sometimes a difference between brands, so use caution.

When a recipe says salt and pepper it generally means a pinch of each, but it is up to the individual to season according to taste. One of the most essential items in a kitchen is a pepper mill. Freshly ground pepper tastes so much better than the pre-ground stuff. If you wish to cut down on your salt intake, use one of the salt substitutes on the market.

If you have a garden why not grow your own herbs? Mint, rosemary, sage, thyme and sorrel all flourish in our climate. Basil does not fair so well, but can still be grown over the summer.

Entertaining

One of the most important reasons for learning how to cook is to be able to entertain. Entertaining gives the ideal opportunity for demonstrating your new-found skills.

In theory, entertaining should be easy. You have learnt how to cook a simple yet elegant dish. You have chosen a good bottle of wine, and you have gathered an interesting selection of friends together. The reality is that you burn the sauce, the wine is oxidised and undrinkable, and you have to stop your guests from a political debate that is about to get messy. Oh yes, entertaining is such fun!

The secret of successful entertaining is forward planning. If you don't plan you are likely to be heading for disaster. If you find entertaining something of a challenge, there are some basic rules that should be adhered to. As the host, you are responsible for your guests' enjoyment. The host has to fulfil a number of roles: besides preparing and cooking the food, the host will have to look after the guests, make introductions, and keep the conversation going if it dries up.

Far too many people dislike entertaining because by the time the guests arrive they are exhausted and stressed after having slaved over a hot stove, only just finishing things off minutes before the guests arrive. You will feel flustered and certainly look flustered. It does not have to be this way. It is good to get into the habit of being so organised when entertaining that you can take the time to relax an hour before the guests arrive.

Planning Tips

The Menu

If you serve good food you are on to a winner. However, there is no point in serving tantalising food if there is only enough for a small portion each. Make sure you cook enough, allowing for seconds. The same applies to the drinks. There can never be enough. Not wishing to encourage excessive drinking, I must admit that entertaining is usually more fun after a few bottles of wine have been emptied.

Plan what you are going to cook well in advance and keep it simple. Don't try to be too adventurous; it is a recipe for disaster. Try cooking a new recipe before the event so you know if it will be suitable, how long it takes to prepare and to cook, as well as the level of competency required. If you don't try it out beforehand, you increase the chance of it going horribly wrong. It is often prudent to play it safe and stick to recipes that you know well.

Presentation

Food always looks and tastes better if an effort is made with the presentation. There is no point in going to a great deal of trouble to prepare a meal then serving it in an unappetising manner. Invest in a couple of attractive serving bowls and dishes, and a set of matching plates. If your cooking is less than palatable, you might then fool the recipient into thinking that it tastes OK.

• Make sure that all the plates, cutlery and glasses are clean. Eating off dirty plates will not make a meal appetising.

• The essence of presentation is to keep the food looking fresh and uncluttered. Plates should not be piled high with food – it makes the person feel obliged to clean their plate and if they have a small appetite this could be a struggle.

• Don't try to combine too many colours or flavours together. Keep it simple and elegant.

• Don't forget to warm the plates and dishes before serving the food.

Wine

This section only pops the cork on a subject that is incredibly fascinating and complex. There is so much that could go in, but this is a cookery book not a wine book so I'll try to keep it brief.

Storing Wine

It is a shame that houses are now built without cellars: not only are they useful for storing all that unwanted junk, or hiding from the wife when she wants you to do yet another menial task, they are also perfect for storing wine. Wine, if it is going to be kept for long periods of time, needs certain conditions or it will rapidly deteriorate. The more expensive the wine, the more care that should be taken.

If you do not have a cellar, then other suitable places are under the stairs or in a spare room. It is essential that the temperature is kept constant. Try not to leave wine in a room where there are constant changes in temperature, for example, in a centrally heated room that is in frequent use.

- The ideal temperature for storing wine is 12 °C, 55 °F.

- Keep the wine away from direct sunlight.

• Lay the wine flat so that the wine makes contact with the cork. This keeps the cork moist and stops it from drying out.

• Don't keep wine in a room that has strong odours as this can taint the wine.

• Try to leave the wine undisturbed.

Serving Wine

To get the most out of a bottle of wine it is important that it is served at the correct temperature.

Red Wine

Most red wines are served at room temperature, around 16 °C, 65 °F. If your wine is cool don't be tempted to speed up the process by placing it near direct heat. Although as a rule red wines are served at the above temperature, there are a few wines that can benefit from being served at a lower temperature, or even chilled, including some wines from the Loire Valley, for instance, St Nicholas de Bourguiel.

There remains an element of disagreement as to whether red wine should be opened in advance of serving. Certain wines definitely require opening well in advance, such as magnums or wines with a high tannin content, while others will not benefit.

White Wine and Rosé

White wine and rosé should be chilled before serving. For perfection the optimum temperature is 7 °C, 45 °F. To get a bottle of wine to temperature will take about two hours in the fridge, or about 30 minutes in an ice bucket. If you have an ice bucket make sure that you put plenty of water in with the ice.

Sparkling Wines

Personally I prefer sparkling wines, such as champagne, as cold as possible. Try to get the temperature down to about 5 °C, 40 °F. This does not mean the wine should be frozen.

Wine Glasses

If you want to get the most from your wine, it is important that you have the right glasses. In theory you should have two types of glass, one for red wine and one for white. A red-wine glass has a wider body than a white-wine glass, as red wine needs a greater area to allow it to breathe. When pouring red wine the glass should only be filled to two-thirds capacity. Never fill a glass up to the brim as it doesn't allow the wine to breath and is awkward to drink.

A white-wine glass should have a long stem so that there is no need to put your hand around the bowl of the glass which would warm it up. The bowl of the glass will be noticeably more slender than the red-wine glass.

Sauces, Stocks and Soups

Sauces

White Sauce

This is one of the most basic sauces to which other ingredients can be added.

Ingredients

1 oz (25 g) butter
¾ oz (20 g) plain flour
½ pint (300 ml) milk
Salt
Pepper

Melt the butter in a small saucepan, but don't let it brown. Then stir in the flour and cook gently for a couple of minutes. The combination of butter and flour is called a roux, and it is also the name of the method of preparation.

Remove the roux from the heat and add a little of the milk. It has to be added gradually otherwise it will end up being lumpy. Stir the milk in until a smooth consistency is achieved, then progressively add the rest of the milk. When all the milk has been added return the pan to the heat and bring to the boil. Simmer for 3 to 5 minutes or until the sauce has thickened, stirring the sauce as it cooks. Season as required.

Cheese Sauce

This sauce is particularly saucy and is used in many of the recipes in this book, such as lasagne.

Ingredients

¾ oz (20 g) butter
¾ oz (20 g) plain flour
½ pint (300 ml) milk
2 oz (50 g) grated cheese
Salt
Pepper

Repeat the method as for the white sauce, except after the sauce has been brought to the boil add the cheese. Stir in the cheese, then simmer until it has completely melted.

Stocks

Although it is easy to be tempted into using a stock cube, you'd be surprised at the improvement in a recipe that uses fresh stock, especially in soups and casseroles. There are three basic stocks which are outlined below, but many others can be made for specialist dishes. Fresh stocks should only be kept in the fridge for a maximum of three days but they are ideal for freezing.

Beef Stock

Ingredients

2 lb (1 kg) beef bones
1 tbsp oil
Water
2 carrots, peeled and chopped
1 onion, peeled and quartered
6 black peppercorns
1 bay leaf
Salt

Heat the oil in a large stock pan, then fry the onions and carrots for five minutes. After frying the vegetables, add the bones, peppercorns, bay leaf and cover with cold water. Bring the pan to the boil slowly, removing any scum that will inevitably rise to the surface. A slotted spoon is useful for removing the scum.

After the stock has been brought to the boil it must be simmered for at least three hours; the longer it is simmered the more intense the flavour of the stock. Whilst the stock is simmering some fat will rise to the surface. This should be removed with a fat skimmer or kitchen towel. If the water level gets low add a little more.

After three or four hours remove the pan from the cooker and strain. When strained, leave to cool and then remove any remaining fat.

Fish Stock

If you are squeamish, then this is one recipe that perhaps you will want to avoid.

Ingredients

2 lb (1 kg) fish trimmings, including bones, tails, head
1 onion, peeled and quartered
1 stick of celery, chopped
1 carrot, peeled and chopped
6 peppercorns

Put all the ingredients in a large saucepan and cover with water, roughly about two pints (1 litre). Bring to the boil, removing any scum that rises to the surface. Simmer for 25 minutes then strain. It is important that the stock is not simmered for any longer than 25 minutes as the fish bones can give off a bitter taste.

Strain the stock through a fine sieve. To increase the flavour of the stock, after it has been strained it can be returned to the pan and reduced.

Chicken Stock

Ingredients

1 whole chicken carcass
1 tbsp oil
1 onion, peeled and quartered
2 carrots, peeled and chopped
3 peppercorns
1 bay leaf
Salt

Prepare the chicken stock using the same method as for the beef stock.

Soups

The recipes for soup are legionary. There are thick, thin, clear, hot, cold ones, and it is possible to produce soup from almost any natural ingredients. A blender is essential if you want a smooth soup.

Carrot and Ginger Soup

This is my favourite of all soups; the ginger gives it a delicious flavour that never fails to impress. Use fresh ginger, but remember to take it out before serving.

Serves 4

Ingredients

1 lb (500 g) carrots, peeled and chopped
1 potato, peeled and chopped
1 piece of fresh root ginger
2 pints (1 litre) water
4 tbsp single cream (optional)
Salt
Pepper

Place the carrots, potato and ginger in a pan and cover with the water. Bring to the boil and then simmer for 20 minutes. Remove from the heat and take out the ginger. Transfer the ingredients into a blender and blend until a smooth consistency is achieved. Season according to taste and stir in the cream if desired.

Tomato Soup

Still one of the most popular soups. Why not try spicing it up by adding a few pinches of chilli powder?

Serves 4

Ingredients

1 lb (500 g) tomatoes
1 onion, peeled and finely chopped
1 clove of garlic, peeled and chopped
1 bay leaf
1 pint (600 ml) water
½ pint (300 ml) milk
1 tbsp oil
Salt
Pepper

Boil some water in a saucepan, then place the tomatoes in it. Remove the pan from the heat and leave for about 5 minutes. This is the best way of skinning a tomato. After this, remove the tomatoes from the water and peel off the skins. Chop into small pieces.

Heat the oil in a saucepan, then fry the tomatoes, onions and garlic slowly for 15 minutes. Add the water and bay leaf, then simmer for 1 hour. If you don't want bits in your soup, sieve the mixture. Otherwise, just add the milk to the tomato mixture, remove the bay leaf and stir. Season. Simmer for about 3 minutes, then serve.

French Onion Soup

The French are passionate about their soups, and most regions have their own speciality soup which reflects the area, the climate and produce. With this recipe there are no firm rules and numerous variations on the same theme occur. This is one soup that benefits from using home-made beef stock.

Serves 4

Ingredients

2 large onions, peeled and thinly sliced
2 pints (1 litre) beef stock
2 tsp flour
1 tbsp oil
4 slices French bread
2 oz (50 g) Gruyère cheese, grated
Salt
Pepper

Heat the oil in a saucepan, then fry the onions slowly for 15 minutes, until they are a golden colour. Stir in the flour and cook for about 5 minutes, stirring the onions constantly. Add the beef stock and bring to the boil. Season and simmer for 25 minutes. Preheat the grill. Divide the cheese onto the slices of bread. When the soup is ready pour it into a serving dish (to be authentic you should have an earthenware tureen), place the slices of bread on top of the soup and put under the grill until the cheese melts. Serve immediately.

Vegetable Soup

At the end of the summer there is usually an abundance of fresh vegetables available from local nurseries. I buy vast quantities of tomatoes and make up batches of tomato sauce and soup that can be frozen and used when needed during the winter.

Serves 4

Ingredients

2 tbsp oil
1 onion, peeled and chopped
1 leek, thinly sliced
2 cabbage leaves, shredded or finely chopped
1 courgette, finely chopped
1 carrot, scraped and sliced
1 tsp mixed herbs
1 bay leaf
2 pints (1 litre) vegetable stock
Salt
Pepper

Heat the oil in a large saucepan, then fry the onions for about 5 minutes or until they have softened. Then add the other vegetables and fry for a further 10 minutes. Add the stock and herbs, then season. Bring to the boil, then simmer for 30 minutes. Remove the bay leaf before serving. If you want a smoother texture liquidise before serving.

Curried Parsnip and Apple Soup

A liquidiser is required for this recipe.

Serves 4

Ingredients

2 tbsp oil
1 large onion, peeled and chopped
1 ½ lb (750 g) parsnips, peeled and chopped
1 apple, peeled and cored
2 tsp medium curry powder
2 pints (1 litre) vegetable stock
Salt
Pepper

Heat the oil in a large saucepan, then fry the onions and curry powder for about 5 minutes until they have softened. Add the apple and the parsnips and fry gently for another 5 minutes. Stir in the stock and bring to the boil, then simmer for 30 minutes. Transfer the soup into a liquidiser and blend until smooth.

Serve with fresh crusty bread. If you don't like the flavour of curry then omit the curry powder.

Gazpacho

This is a thin chilled soup that is very refreshing on a hot summer's evening. A blender is needed for this recipe. I often add a dash of Tabasco sauce, but this is optional.

Serves 4

Ingredients

8 oz (225 g) ripe tomatoes, skinned
½ green pepper, deseeded and chopped
½ red pepper, deseeded and chopped
½ cucumber
1 pint (600 ml) tomato juice
1 onion, peeled and chopped
1 clove of garlic, peeled and chopped
2 tbsp olive oil
1 tbsp tarragon vinegar
1 tbsp fresh chives
1 tbsp fresh parsley
Salt
Pepper

Chop all the vegetables into chunks and put aside a little of each for the garnish. Place all the ingredients except for the oil into a blender for 2 minutes or so. Then add the oil and seasoning, and place in the fridge for at least 3 hours. A few ice cubes can be added to speed up this process, but don't add too many as it will make the soup weak. Serve with the reserved vegetables on top.

Chilled Cucumber Soup

This is another soup that is ideal for serving during the summer months.

Serves 4

Ingredients

2 cucumbers, peeled and sliced
1 tbsp flour
1 pint (600 ml) chicken stock
½ pint (300 ml) water
½ tsp grated nutmeg
¼ pint (150 ml) single cream
1 bay leaf
1 tbsp fresh mint, chopped
Salt
Pepper

Place the cucumber into a saucepan with the water and cook until tender. Remove from the heat and then put in a blender for a minute or two until smooth. Return the cucumber to the saucepan and stir in the flour. Add the stock, seasoning and bay leaf then slowly bring to the boil. Simmer for 5 minutes then cool and strain. Once strained stir in the cream and chill in the fridge for a couple of hours. Serve the soup with a decoration of mint.

Pumpkin Soup

This recipe requires a liquidiser and a little enthusiasm for Halloween night.

Serves 4

Ingredients

1 ½ lb (750 g) pumpkin flesh, cut into cubes
½ pint (300 ml) milk
4 oz (100 g) butter
Salt
Pepper

Melt the butter in a saucepan, then fry the pumpkin until it is soft and mushy. Season, then add milk and put into a liquidiser for a minute. Put the liquid back into a saucepan and heat through, but do not boil.

Starters and Nibbles

Deep Fried Camembert

Serves 2

Ingredients

1 Camembert cheese
Dried white breadcrumbs
1 egg, beaten
Vegetable oil

Cut the Camembert into four, then dip in the egg, followed by a roll in the breadcrumbs, making sure the pieces are evenly coated. Put on a plate and place in the fridge for 30 minutes.

Heat the oil in a deep fryer until it begins to smoke. Test the temperature by dropping a breadcrumb into the oil. It should sizzle as soon as it hits the surface. When the oil is at the correct temperature fry the Camembert until golden. Drain and then serve with redcurrant sauce.

Smoked Salmon Salad

Serves 4

Ingredients

Mixed salad
4 oz (100 g) smoked salmon
1 lemon, cut into wedges
Salt
Pepper
Olive oil

Arrange the mixed salad on four small plates so that the plates are covered. Cut the salmon into small pieces then place on the salad leaves. Drizzle lightly with olive oil, then season. Serve with the lemon wedges.

Moules Marinières

Serves 4

Ingredients

4 lb (2 kg) mussels
2 cloves garlic, peeled and finely chopped
4 shallots, peeled and finely chopped
2 tbsp chopped parsley
1 oz (25 g) butter
1 pint (600 ml) white wine
Salt
Pepper

Scrub the mussels and remove the beards that are usually attached to them. If there are any mussels that are already open or cracked discard them. Put the shallots, wine, garlic and parsley into a large saucepan and simmer for 5 minutes. Add the mussels, turn up the heat and cook for about 5 minutes. Then add the butter and cook for another 10 minutes. Whilst the mussels are cooking shake the pan a couple of times. This helps the mussels to open and ensures they are cooked evenly.

When cooked, remove any mussels that have not opened. Season and then serve with the cooking juices. If a slightly stronger tasting sauce is required, reduce the sauce by boiling it rapidly for a few minutes. The mussels should be served immediately with a little chopped parsley on top.

Mini Sausages with Honey and Rosemary

In cooking it is often the simple dishes that can be the most rewarding, and this is one such dish. Delicious.

Serves 4

Ingredients

Pack of mini sausages
Handful of fresh rosemary
3 tbsp runny honey

Arrange the sausages in a baking dish, prick with a fork, spoon on the honey, then place the rosemary on top. I find that slightly crushing the rosemary gives a stronger taste to the sausages. Bake in the oven on Gas Mark 6 (220 °C, 425 °F) for about 40 minutes, turning occasionally so they brown evenly. If you are in a hurry stick the sausages under the grill.

Goat's Cheese Salad

Even if you are into strong cheese, a ripe goat's cheese can bring tears to your eyes.

Serves 4

Ingredients

4 small goat's cheeses
Mixed salad
2 tbs of olive oil
Salt
Pepper

Arrange the salad on four small plates. Heat the oil in a small frying pan and then add the cheese. Lightly fry the cheese until it gets close to melting. Use a pan slice to remove the cheese from the pan and then place on top of the salad. Any oil that remains in the pan can be poured over the salad. Finally season.

Mushrooms with Garlic Butter

Serves 4

Ingredients

4 oz (100 g) mushrooms
3 oz (75 g) butter
2 cloves of garlic, peeled and finely chopped

Remove the stalks of the mushrooms, then wipe. Mix the butter and the garlic together with a fork and then spread on top of the mushrooms. Bake in the oven for 15 minutes on Gas Mark 5 (200 °C, 400 °F).

Garlic Bread

Serves 4

Ingredients

French stick
4 oz (100 g) butter
2 cloves of garlic
Tinfoil

Put the butter in a small mixing bowl. Finely chop the garlic and add to the butter, blending it in with a fork. Slice the French stick at 2-inch intervals, without actually severing it, and spread some of the butter on both sides of each slit. Then close up the gaps and wrap the loaf in foil. Place in the oven and cook for 15 to 20 minutes at Gas Mark 5 (200 °C, 400 °F).

Hummus

This is a dip of Middle Eastern origin, and it is very easy to make. Serve with pitta bread. Note that a blender is needed for this recipe.

Ingredients

1 can of chick peas
2 cloves of garlic, peeled and finely chopped
1 tbsp tahini
Juice of one lemon
2 tbsp olive oil
½ tsp ground cumin
Paprika

Put all the ingredients in a blender, except the paprika, and let them have it! Switch off when a smooth consistency has been achieved. Then put in a dish and chill for an hour or two. Dust with paprika before serving. If your hummus is too thick stir in a tablespoon or two of natural yogurt or water.

Guacamole

Serves 3 to 4

Ingredients

2 ripe avocados
3 tbsp lemon juice
1 tbsp olive oil
1 clove of garlic, peeled and crushed
Pinch of chilli powder
Salt
Pepper

Peel the avocados and remove the stones. Mash the flesh with a fork and add the other ingredients. Season to taste and serve with tortilla chips, raw vegetables or on toast.

Tapenade

If you spend any time in Provence you are bound to come across certain dishes for which the region is celebrated and Tapenade is one of them. The name comes from the word 'tapeno', which is French for capers. Serve on toast or with crackers.

Serves 4

Ingredients

12 black olives, stoned
6 anchovy fillets
2 oz (50 g) tinned tuna
3 tbsp capers
1 clove garlic, peeled and crushed
3 tbsp olive oil
1 tbsp cognac

Put the olives, anchovies, capers, garlic and tuna in a food processor and blend to a paste. Then add the olive oil and cognac and mix well. The amount of olive oil used is only a guide; it depends on the required consistency as to how much is used.

Aïoli

This is one Provençal recipe that lacks the characteristic vibrant colours normally associated with its cuisine. What it might lack in colour it makes up for in flavour – this recipe is a knockout. It is rarely served in this country, possibly as a result of its high garlic content. You are missing out if you don't try this favourite of our Gallic chums. Aïoli should ideally be served with hard-boiled eggs and raw tomatoes, and freshly cooked vegetables such as courgettes and French beans. Serve on a large platter dish.

Ingredients

6 cloves of garlic
2 egg yolks
Juice of 1 lemon
½ pint (300 ml) olive oil
Salt
Pepper

Using a pestle and mortar, crush the garlic with a pinch of salt into a fine paste. Transfer the garlic into a mixing bowl then add the egg yolks. The next stage is the same as when making mayonnaise (see page 81); the oil must be added very slowly and the mixture stirred constantly. When all the oil is added, season and add the lemon juice.

Salads and Salad Dressings

The use of dressings can add life to even the most miserable salad. By making your own dressings you can fine-tune them according to your own personal tastes. It should be remembered that a dressing should not swamp a salad. The salad should be coated, not bathed. It is possible to buy ready-prepared dressings but they rarely match those that are home-made.

French Dressing

Most people are familiar with French dressing, also commonly referred to by the French name vinaigrette.

There are many variations of French dressing, and most people have their own favourite combinations. Oil and vinegar are the primary ingredients to which herbs or flavourings can be added. Olive oil is a must for an authentic-tasting dressing; vegetable oil, although much cheaper, will not taste the same, and use a wine vinegar, not malt. As with most recipes, even ones that only contain two ingredients, there are disagreements as to the correct proportions of oil and vinegar. This is yet another one of those daft arguments; the proportions should be based upon personal preference. Usually the dressing is 4 parts oil to 1 part vinegar, although you might prefer a less acidic flavour and use 6 parts oil.

Ingredients

4 tbsp olive oil
1 tbsp white wine vinegar
Salt
Pepper

What could be easier? Put the oil, vinegar, salt and pepper in a small screw-top jar and shake until the two liquids have combined. After a while the oil and vinegar will separate again.

If you want a dressing out of the ordinary try adding a little mustard or fresh herbs such as basil, mint, parsley or chives. An alternative to using vinegar is to use lemon juice.

Garlic Dressing

Make as above, but add half a finely crushed clove of garlic.

Mayonnaise

Ingredients

2 egg yolks
2 tsp white wine vinegar
½ pint (300 ml) olive oil
Squirt of lemon juice
1 tsp smooth French mustard
Salt
Pepper

Put the egg yolks into a mixing bowl with the mustard and mix together. Slowly begin to add the olive oil. The main problem with making mayonnaise is that it can curdle if the oil is added too quickly. Mayonnaise is time consuming to make, but it is essential to take care. A fine drizzle of oil is needed and has to be controlled with total precision. Hold the bottle of oil at the bottom in the palm of your hand, this gives more control. Using a balloon whisk, beat the yolks and the oil together. You will notice that the colour is quite yellow in comparison with the bought variety, but this is the way it should be. Keep whisking the mayonnaise until all the oil is added, then add the vinegar, lemon juice, salt and pepper, and mix together. Taste and adjust the flavourings to suit.

Mayonnaise can be produced in a food processor, but again fine control is required and the result is not as good. Put all the ingredients, bar the oil, in the processor and switch on, then add the oil slowly.

Tomato and Feta Salad

Serves 4

Ingredients

6 ripe tomatoes
4 oz (100 g) feta cheese
10 black olives
Olive oil
Salt
Pepper

Slice the tomatoes and arrange on a flat plate or platter dish. Cut the cheese into cubes or crumble into small pieces and place on top of the tomatoes. Arrange the olives on top, season, then drizzle with oil.

Alsace Salad

This is one of my favourite salads. Appetites tend to be large in this region of France, and, being close to the border with Germany, much of the cuisine is influenced by both countries. This is not the region to visit if you are attempting to lose weight.

Serves 2

Ingredients

1 lettuce
4 rashers of bacon, cut into pieces
2 eggs
2 tomatoes, quartered
2 tbsp oil
Salt
Pepper

Heat the oil in a frying pan and fry the bacon. With this particular recipe the bacon pieces need to be verging on crispness, but don't let them burn. When they are cooked put them aside in a separate dish or bowl. Clear the pan of any debris then fry the eggs. Whilst the eggs are cooking arrange the lettuce in a serving dish with the tomatoes and the bacon. When the eggs are cooked let them cool for a minute and then place on top of the salad, then season.

Pasta Salad

Serves 3 to 4

Ingredients

4 oz (100 g) pasta quills or shells
½ red pepper, deseeded and chopped
½ green pepper, deseeded and chopped
8 oz (225 g) tin of tuna
3 tomatoes, sliced
3 tbsp double cream
Pepper

Boil some water in a saucepan and cook the pasta for about 15 minutes or until it is tender, then drain.

Drain the oil from the tuna then mix all the ingredients together in a serving bowl and season.

Tomato and Onion Salad

A typical Provençal salad, so popular that anyone indigenous to the area would give their best goat for just a taste of it (the salad, not the goat).

Serves 4

Ingredients

4 fresh tomatoes
1 onion
Fresh basil
Pepper
Salt
French dressing

Peel the onion and slice fairly thinly. Slice the tomatoes and arrange them on a large plate or dish. Place the onion pieces between the tomato slices. Decorate with the basil leaves, and season with plenty of freshly ground pepper and salt. Pour the French dressing over the top.

Salad Niçoise

This salad is legendary in Provence. As with many French recipes there are numerous variations on the same theme, so there is never a 'right' way!

Serves 4

Ingredients

1 lettuce
3 ripe tomatoes
½ small onion, thinly sliced
10 French beans cooked and cooled
3 eggs
8 oz (225 g) tin of tuna
Small tin of anchovies
10 olives
French dressing

Hard boil the eggs for 8 minutes, then place in a bowl of cold water. Wash the lettuce and arrange the leaves in a large serving bowl, then add the onions and tuna (drain the oil first).

Quarter the tomatoes and place them on top of the lettuce, with the beans. Shell the eggs, cut them into quarters, and arrange them neatly on top of the tuna. Pour the dressing over the salad, and add the olives and anchovies. Other ingredients that are sometimes used include radishes and peppers.

Italian Pepper Salad

There are many ways of serving peppers but this simple recipe is one of the best.

Serves 4

Ingredients

4 large peppers (mixture of colours)
4 tbsp olive oil
1 tsp capers
Salt
Pepper

Heat the oven to the highest setting possible, and then place the peppers on a tray on the top shelf. They should stay in the oven for 20 to 30 minutes after the oven is up to temperature. After about 15 minutes turn the peppers over so they are evenly cooked.

Remove from the oven and put the peppers in a clean polythene bag and tie the ends together. Leave the peppers in the bag for at least 15 minutes then remove and peel off the skins. Make sure all the skin is removed, as when it is burnt it has a very strong flavour and can taint the dish.

After removing the skin, remove the stems and seeds then cut into strips. Place the peppers in a serving dish with the capers, drizzle with the oil and then season. There will normally be some residue from the peppers in the polythene bag that can be added to the dish for extra flavour.

Potato Salad

Serves 4

Ingredients

10 medium potatoes, peeled, or 20 new potatoes
Mayonnaise
Salt
Pepper

If you are using new potatoes the skins can be left on, just scrub them. Place the potatoes in boiling water for 15 minutes or until a knife will pass through the centre fairly easily.

After the potatoes have cooled, cut into halves or quarters, depending on their size. If you are using small new potatoes they can be left whole. Place in a bowl and dollop some mayonnaise on top. Mix together and season.

Chopped fresh chives can be added if you like.

Cucumber Salad

Cucumbers are very high in water content and are refreshing to eat.

Serves 4

Ingredients

1 large cucumber
1 tbsp white wine vinegar
1 tsp sugar
1 tbsp olive oil
2 tbsp chopped fresh chives
Salt
Pepper

Peel the cucumber and slice as thinly as possible. A mandolin is ideal for producing wafer-thin slices.

Arrange the slices of cucumber on a flat plate and sprinkle generously with salt. Place another plate of a similar size on top and press down gently.

Leave in the fridge for 1 hour. Remove from the fridge and pour away the water that has been extracted. Mix the vinegar, oil and sugar together, then pour over the cucumber. Season, then sprinkle the chopped chives on top.

Tabbouleh

Bulgur wheat is made from wheat that has been boiled, dried, then ground. As an ingredient it is widely used in countries like Morocco and Tunisia. Tabbouleh is a perfect dish for serving at a buffet supper, where it makes an interesting contrast to traditional salads.

Serves 4

Ingredients

6 oz (150 g) bulgur wheat
3 tbsp olive oil
½ cucumber, chopped
2 tomatoes, peeled and chopped
1 bunch of spring onions
1 bunch of parsley
8 mint leaves, chopped
Juice of one lemon
Salt
Pepper

Place the bulgur wheat in a saucepan of water. Bring to the boil, then simmer gently for 10 to 15 minutes until tender. Drain, then allow to cool.

Finely chop the parsley and the spring onions. Place the bulgur in a serving bowl, add the olive oil, parsley, mint, tomato, cucumber, spring onions, lemon juice, salt and pepper. Mix together thoroughly.

MEAT

Beef

Shepherd's Pie

This popular dish is supposed to use leftover beef from a Sunday roast, but minced beef is an adequate substitute for those not indulging in a roast. This recipe has many variations: I prefer to use the one that includes tomatoes, but try both and see which one you like.

Serves 3 to 4

Ingredients

2 tbsp oil
1 onion, peeled and chopped
1 clove of garlic, peeled and finely chopped
1 lb (500 g) minced beef
1 tin of tomatoes (optional)
1 tbsp tomato purée
1 tsp mixed herbs
5 medium potatoes, peeled
Butter
Milk
Salt
Pepper

Heat the oil in a largish saucepan, add the onion and garlic, and fry for 3 to 4 minutes. Add the meat and cook for another 10 minutes, then add the tomatoes, tomato purée, mixed herbs, salt and pepper, and simmer for 15 minutes.

While this is simmering, cook the potatoes (test them with a knife – the knife should pass through the potato easily), then mash them with a knob of butter and a drop of milk. Put the meat in an ovenproof dish and cover with the potato, then put under the grill until the potato turns a golden brown.

Moussaka

Serves 4

Ingredients

1 large aubergine, sliced
2 large potatoes, parboiled and sliced
2 onions, peeled and chopped
1 tin of tomatoes
1 tbsp tomato purée
1 clove of garlic, crushed and finely chopped
1 lb (500 g) minced beef or lamb
2 tbsp oil
1 oz (25 g) butter
1 oz (25 g) flour
¾ pint (375 ml) milk
4 oz (100 g) grated cheese
Salt
Pepper

Sprinkle the aubergines generously with salt and leave for 30 minutes. Then rinse and pat dry with kitchen paper. Heat a tablespoon of oil in a frying pan and fry the aubergines until they are soft. Then place on a piece of kitchen towel to absorb the fat. Put some more oil in the frying pan if needed and fry the onions, garlic, and meat. After about 10 minutes, season, and add the tomatoes and purée.

Grease a casserole dish with either butter or oil, and fill it with alternate layers of aubergine and meat, finishing with a layer of sliced potatoes.

To make the cheese sauce, melt the butter in a saucepan, add the flour, and mix together. Remove from the heat, and very gradually add the milk. Return to the heat and boil until the sauce thickens, then remove from the heat and add 3 oz (75 g) of the cheese. Pour the cheese sauce over the top of the aubergine, and sprinkle the rest of the cheese on top.

Bake for 40 minutes on Gas Mark 5 (200 °C, 400 °F).

Goulash

This dish traditionally uses veal, but beef is normally used due to the controversy surrounding the methods by which veal is produced.

Serves 4

Ingredients

2 tbsp oil
1 large onion, peeled and chopped
1 lb (500 g) potatoes, peeled and sliced
1 clove of garlic, peeled and finely chopped
1 lb (500 g) cubed stewing beef
1 red pepper, deseeded and chopped
1 green pepper, deseeded and chopped
½ tsp caraway seeds
1 tbsp paprika
1 tsp mixed herbs
1 beef stock cube
¾ pint (450 ml) boiling water
4 oz (100 g) sliced mushrooms
1 tin of tomatoes
¼ pint (150 ml) soured cream (optional)
Salt
Pepper

Heat the oil in a casserole dish or a large saucepan, then fry the onions and garlic for a couple of minutes. Add the meat, peppers, tomatoes, mixed herbs, paprika, caraway seeds, salt and pepper, and cook for about 5 minutes.

Dissolve the stock cube in the boiling water and add to the above. Simmer for about 40 minutes, then add the potatoes and cook for another 40 minutes. After about 30 minutes add the mushrooms. If they are added any earlier they will be overcooked and go mushy.

Before serving add the soured cream, if required.

Chilli Con Carne

The chilli can be made as hot as required, but remember that even though you may love to sweat, your guests might prefer it a little milder.

Serves 4

Ingredients

2 tbsp oil
3 tsp chilli powder
1 lb (500 g) minced beef or stewing steak
1 large onion, peeled and chopped
2 cloves of garlic, peeled and finely chopped
¼ pint (150 ml) beef stock
1 tin of tomatoes
1 tin of kidney beans, drained
1 tsp oregano
1 tbsp tomato purée
1 glass of red wine (optional)
Salt
Pepper

After frying the onions, chilli powder and garlic in the oil for about 5 minutes, mix in the mince. Cook the mince for about 10 minutes, stirring constantly to stop it burning. Add the other ingredients, except the kidney beans, varying the amounts of seasoning according to taste. Bring to the boil then simmer for about 20 minutes (the longer the better). Add the kidney beans 5 minutes before serving.

Serve with rice or jacket potatoes.

Beef Stew

Serves 4

Ingredients

1 lb (500 g) stewing steak
1 onion, peeled and roughly chopped
1 clove of garlic, peeled and finely chopped
1 ½ oz (40 g) flour
1 pint (600 ml) beef stock
3 carrots, scraped and chopped
1 bay leaf
2 tbsp oil
Salt
Pepper

Put the oil in a casserole dish and fry the onions and garlic for 5 minutes. Cut the meat into 1-inch (2.5 cm) pieces and roll them in the flour with a little salt and pepper. Fry for 5 minutes or until brown, and add to the onion. Add the rest of the flour to the pan and fry gently. Add the stock and boil until it thickens. Pour the sauce over the meat, add the bay leaf and carrots, and bake at Gas Mark 4 (180 °C, 350 °F) for one to two hours. Remove the bay leaf before serving.

Corned Beef Hash

This recipe proves that simple, inexpensive ingredients combined can create a tasty meal.

Serves 4

Ingredients

2 tbsp oil
1 tin of corned beef
1 large onion, peeled and chopped
Milk
Butter
4 large potatoes
Salt
Pepper

Peel the potatoes and chop them into quarters. Place the potatoes in a saucepan of boiling water and boil for about 20 minutes or until tender. Drain them and mash with a little milk and butter.

Whilst the potatoes are cooking fry the onions in a large frying pan with the oil for about 5 minutes or until they are golden. Open the tin of beef and chop up into small pieces and add to the onion.

Heat the beef through which will take about 5 minutes and then add the mashed potato. Fry the mixture until the potato turns slightly crispy, but not burnt.

Best served with baked beans.

Roast Beef and Yorkshire Pudding

Serves 2 to 20
(according to whether you have a small joint or a whole cow)

Ingredients

1 joint of beef (topside)
4 tbsp vegetable oil
Salt
Pepper

For the Yorkshire Pudding:

Serves 4

4 oz (100 g) plain flour
1 egg, beaten
½ pint (300 ml) milk, or milk and water
Oil
A pinch of salt

Before throwing away the packaging for your joint, note how much it weighs. Allow 20 minutes cooking time per lb, plus 20 minutes on top, all at Gas Mark 7 (230 °C, 450 °F). This will cook the meat 'English style', i.e. with little or no blood seeping out. If you prefer it 'rare', cook for about 15 minutes less.

Put the joint in a roasting tin and pour the oil over the top and the sides. Season with the salt and pepper, and stick in the pre-heated oven.

The joint must be basted two or three times.

When the meat is cooked, carve the joint and serve with fresh vegetables. Gravy can be made from the juices in the roasting tin.

For the Yorkshire pudding, mix the salt and flour together in a mixing bowl, then make a 'well' in the flour and add the egg. Mix in the flour carefully, adding a little milk until all the flour is mixed in, then add the remaining milk. Beat the mixture for a few minutes until it is smooth. Pour a teaspoon of oil into the individual patty tins, then add 2 tablespoons of the mixture into each. Bake for about 15 minutes or until the puddings have risen and browned.

Lasagne

This is one of everybody's favourite Italian dishes. See the vegetarian section for an alternative recipe.

Serves 4

Ingredients

2 tbsp oil
1 large onion, peeled and chopped
2 cloves of garlic, peeled and finely chopped
1 lb (500 g) minced beef
1 tin of tomatoes
¼ pint (150 ml) beef stock
2 tbsp tomato purée
2 tsp oregano
Salt
Pepper
1 packet of lasagne (the 'no pre-cooking required' type)

For the cheese sauce:

1 oz (25 g) butter
2 oz (50 g) flour
1 pint (600 ml) milk
6 oz (150 g) cheese, grated

After heating the oil in a large saucepan add the onion and garlic and cook for 5 minutes. Add the mince and cook thoroughly. Then add the tomatoes, oregano, beefstock, tomato purée and seasoning. After bringing to the boil, simmer for 15 to 20 minutes.

While the meat sauce is reducing, prepare the cheese sauce. Melt the butter in a saucepan and then add the flour, stirring constantly. Remove from the heat and add the milk in stages. If the milk is added in one go, you end up with lumps in the sauce. After adding the milk, bring to the boil and add the cheese, saving a bit for the top. Then simmer for 3 or 4 minutes; the sauce should now begin to thicken.

OK, so your sauce has not thickened: don't panic! Try adding a bit more flour, but sieve it first if you can. Lumpiness can be rectified by pouring the mixture through a sieve.

Find a shallow baking dish and grease it, then add a layer of meat sauce followed by a layer of lasagne, followed by a layer of cheese sauce. Continue this formation until you have used up your mixtures, making sure you finish with the cheese sauce. As well as sprinkling cheese on top, fresh tomato can be added.

Bake on the middle shelf of a pre-heated oven at Gas Mark 6 (220 °C, 425 °F) for 30 to 40 minutes.

Spaghetti Bolognese

Serves 4

Ingredients

2 tbsp oil
1 lb (500 g) minced beef
1 onion, peeled and chopped
1 tin of tomatoes
4 oz (100 g) mushrooms, washed and sliced
2 cloves of garlic, finely chopped
1 carrot, grated
3 rashers of streaky bacon, cut into small pieces
1 glass of red wine (optional)
1 tbsp tomato purée
¾ pint (450 ml) beef stock
2 tsp oregano
Salt
Pepper

Put the oil into a large saucepan and heat. Add the onions and garlic, and fry gently for 5 minutes, being careful not to burn them. Add the minced beef and continue frying for a further 10 minutes. Add the other ingredients.

After your sauce has reduced, which takes around 20 minutes, serve with a pasta of your choice – it doesn't have to be spaghetti.

Steaks

The most popular steaks are rump, fillet and sirloin. Fillet is the most tender and lean, but unfortunately the most expensive. Rump steak has a wonderful flavour but is not as tender.

Steaks are best grilled or fried.

To grill

Brush the steaks with butter and season with black pepper. Make sure the grill is hot before you cook the steaks. Grill each side for 3 to 4 minutes. If you want the steaks dripping with blood cook for slightly less time or eat raw. If you like your steaks well done cook for 5 to 6 minutes on each side.

To fry

Heat a small amount of oil, preferably in a non-stick frying pan. Wait till the pan gets very hot then put in the steak. Fry quickly for a couple of minutes to seal in the flavour. Turn down the heat, cook for 5 minutes for 'rare', 5 to 7 minutes for medium and 15 minutes for charcoal. Try to turn the steak over only once.

The above times for both grilling and frying will depend on the thickness of the steak.

Serve the steaks with fried or new potatoes, a salad or fresh vegetables.

Beef Stroganoff

Serves 4

Ingredients

1 lb (500 g) fillet steak
1 large onion, peeled and chopped
1 clove of garlic, peeled and finely chopped
4 oz (100 g) mushrooms, sliced
2 oz (50 g) butter
2 tbsp brandy
½ pint (300 ml) soured cream
Salt
Pepper

Bash the steak with a rolling pin to flatten it out, but don't get too carried away. Cut into strips ½ inch (1.5 cm) wide and 2 inches (2.5 cm) long. Fry the steak in the butter for 3 or 4 minutes, then remove from the pan and put in a bowl.

Fry the onions and garlic for 5 minutes, then add the mushrooms and cook until they have softened. Season and put the meat back in the pan. Cook for about 10 minutes, stirring occasionally to prevent burning.

Before serving, add the soured cream and the brandy and heat through. Do not allow to boil, otherwise the cream will curdle.

Burgers

If you haven't made your own before why not give it a go?

Serves 4

Ingredients

1 lb (500 g) minced beef
1 onion, peeled and finely chopped
2 oz (50 g) breadcrumbs
1 tbsp chopped fresh parsley
Dash of Worcester sauce
1 tbsp olive oil
Salt
Pepper

Throw all the ingredients in a bowl, mix together using your hands, and divide the mixture into 4 portions. Shape each portion into something that resembles a burger. Cook for about 4 or 5 minutes on each side, or until brown. To produce a more exotic burger try adding chopped garlic and herbs.

Pork

Pork Provençal

Serves 4

Ingredients

4 pork steaks or chops
1 onion, chopped and peeled
1 clove of garlic, peeled and finely chopped
1 tin of tomatoes
1 red pepper, deseeded and finely chopped
2 tsp herbes de Provence
1 finely chopped courgette
4 slices of cheddar cheese
2 tbsp oil
Salt
Pepper

Fry the onion and garlic in the oil for about 5 minutes. When these have cooked, add the tomatoes, red pepper, courgette, herbs, salt and pepper. Let the sauce simmer for 20 minutes. After 10 minutes, grill the pork on foil, turning once. When it is nearly cooked put some sauce and the slices of cheese on the pork and grill until the cheese begins to melt.

Serve with potatoes, fresh vegetables and the rest of the sauce.

Pork Stir-Fry

Serves 2

Ingredients

2 tbsp oil
8 oz (225 g) diced pork
1 green pepper, deseeded and chopped
1 onion, peeled and chopped
1 tsp chilli powder
1 clove of garlic, peeled and sliced
1 tbsp soy sauce
Salt
Pepper

Heat the oil in a large frying pan or wok, then fry the onions and the garlic for 3 to 4 minutes. Add the pepper, soy sauce and the pork. Fry until the pork is cooked, then season. This should take about 10 minutes, depending on the size of the meat pieces. Serve with rice.

Courgette and Bacon Bake

Serves 4

Ingredients

2 tbsp oil
2 lb (1 kg) courgettes, sliced
4 oz (100 g) bacon, cut into pieces
5 oz (125 g) grated cheddar cheese
4 eggs
¾ pint (450 ml) milk
Salt
Pepper

Fry the courgettes for 4 to 5 minutes, then add the bacon and fry for another couple of minutes. Beat the eggs together with the milk, add most of the cheese, reserving some for the topping, and season. Grease a baking dish and layer the courgettes and bacon until they are used up. Pour the egg and cheese mixture over the courgettes, put the rest of the cheese on top, and bake at Gas Mark 4 (180 °C, 350 °F) for 30 minutes or until golden.

Roast Pork and Apple Sauce

Ingredients

1 joint of pork
4 tbsp vegetable oil
Salt
Pepper

For the Apple Sauce:

1 lb (500 g) cooking apples, peeled, cored and
sliced
3 tbsp water
Juice of half a lemon
½ oz (15 g) butter
2 tsp sugar

Pork must be cooked for a little longer than beef, for it is essential that pork is well cooked. Before throwing away the packaging for your joint, note how much it weighs. Allow 25 minutes per pound plus 25 minutes over at Gas Mark 7 (230 °C, 450 °F). Put the joint in a roasting tin and pour the oil over the top and the sides. Season with the salt and pepper, and stick in the pre-heated oven. Baste the joint every 20 minutes.

For the apple sauce, put the apples in a saucepan with the lemon juice, water, sugar and butter and simmer gently until the apples are soft. Take care not to burn the apples. If you want a smooth sauce put the mixture in a blender for a minute. If the sauce is too bitter add a little more sugar.

Tomato and Ham Pasta Sauce

Serves 4

Ingredients

2 tbsp olive oil
1 tin of tomatoes
1 onion, peeled and chopped
4 slices of ham, cut into strips
2 cloves of garlic, peeled and finely chopped
1 tbsp tomato purée
1 glass of red wine (optional)
2 tsp oregano or mixed herbs
Salt
Pepper

Heat the oil in a saucepan and fry the onions and garlic for about 5 minutes. Then add the other ingredients and simmer for 20 minutes. Serve with a pasta of your choice.

Pork and Cider Casserole

Serves 4

Ingredients

2 tbsp oil
1 large onion, peeled and chopped
2 cloves of garlic, peeled and finely chopped
1 tin of tomatoes
1 tbsp tomato purée
2 tsp herbes de Provence
1 green pepper, deseeded and chopped
1 courgette, sliced
4 pork chops
1 pint (600 ml) dry cider
1 mug of macaroni
½ mug of frozen peas
Salt
Pepper

Heat the oil in a large casserole dish, then fry the onion, garlic and green pepper for about 5 minutes. Then add the pork chops and fry on both sides for a couple of minutes. Add the tomatoes, purée, herbs, courgette, seasoning and cider then bring to the boil.

Simmer for about 40 minutes, adding the macaroni 10 minutes before serving and the peas 5 minutes after the pasta. Check to see if the macaroni is cooked before serving.

If the casserole begins to get a little dry add some water or more cider.

Carbonara

I'm not sure if this is the traditional recipe for the dish, but it tastes good to me.

Serves 3 to 4

Ingredients

1 tbsp oil
14 oz (400 g) tagliatelle
4 rashers of streaky bacon, cut into small pieces
4 egg yolks
3 oz (75 g) grated Parmesan cheese
4 tbsp double cream
Lots of fresh black pepper
A pinch of salt

Cook the pasta according to the instructions on the back of the packet. Fry the bacon in the oil for 4 to 5 minutes. When the pasta is cooked, strain and then return to the pan. Then mix in the cheese, bacon, egg, cream and seasoning. Heat gently for about a minute until the cheese has melted, then serve immediately with more black pepper.

Lamb

Roast Lamb and Mint Sauce

Ingredients

1 joint of lamb
4 tbsp vegetable oil
Salt
Pepper

For the Mint Sauce:

1 cup of fresh mint
2 tbsp vinegar
2 tbsp caster sugar
2 tbsp hot water

Before throwing away the packaging for your joint, note how much it weighs. Cook for 20 minutes per pound and 20 minutes over on Gas Mark 7 (230 °C, 450 °F). Put the joint in a roasting tin and pour the oil over the top and the sides. Season with the salt and pepper, and stick in the pre-heated oven. Baste every 20 minutes. After removing from oven, let the meat 'rest' for 10 minutes before carving.

For the mint sauce, wash the mint then remove the leaves. Finely chop the leaves and place in a bowl with the sugar. Pour on the hot water and stir. Leave for 5 minutes or until the sugar has dissolved. Add the vinegar and leave to infuse for at least 2 hours.

Lamb Casserole

Serves 4

Ingredients

2 tbsp oil
4 lamb chops
1 onion, peeled and sliced
2 leeks, sliced
8 oz (225 g) carrots, scraped and chopped
4 oz (100 g) peas
1 pint (600 ml) beef or vegetable stock
Salt
Pepper

Heat the oil in a frying pan then fry the chops for a couple of minutes on each side. Then add the onion, carrots and leek, and fry for a few more minutes. Transfer into a casserole dish, season, and pour the stock over. Put a lid on the dish and place in the oven on Gas Mark 4 (180 °C, 350 °F) for about 1 hour. Add the peas about 10 minutes before serving.

Glazed Lamb Chops

The chops need to be marinated for several hours but they only take a few minutes to cook.

Serves 4

Ingredients

1 tbsp oil
4 thick lamb chops
2 wine glasses of sherry
1 tbsp mint sauce
2 tsp dark brown sugar
Salt
Pepper

Place the lamb chops in a bowl and mix all the ingredients together. Leave the chops in the marinade for at least 6 hours in the fridge.

To cook the chops, take them out of the marinade. Heat the oil in a frying pan and fry the chops for a few minutes on each side. They should be served still pink in the middle.

When they are cooked, remove from the pan, pour in the remaining marinade and reduce by bringing to the boil. Pour the sauce over the chops and serve with fresh vegetables.

Lamb with Honey and Rosemary

Buy the thickest lamb chops available.

Serves 4

Ingredients

4 lamb chops
4 sprigs fresh rosemary
2 tbsp runny honey

Pierce the lamb chops using a sharp knife and insert small pieces of rosemary. Put in a mixing bowl and spoon over the honey, so that the chops are evenly coated.

Place the chops in a pan or on the barbecue and cook until the meat is to your liking.

Sausages

The banger is an amazing invention: versatile, timeless, classless and sausage-shaped. After all these years it still provides a cheap, simple and cholesterolly dangerous meal. Sausages come in various types, the most popular variants containing either pork or beef but it is possible to buy more exotic varieties made from venison or wild rabbit. The price will depend on their fat content – the cheapest might be almost pure tubes of fat. Handmade sausages can still be found at some local butcher shops.

The usual methods for cooking sausages are frying and grilling. For those who want to minimise the relative unhealthiness of the sausage, grilling is the better way to choose.

To grill
Remember to prick the sausages, then grill for about 10 minutes on each side, on a medium heat.

To fry
Prick the sausages all over with a fork. Heat some oil in a frying pan, and fry the sausages for 15 to 20 minutes. Turn them regularly when cooking to make sure they brown and cook evenly.

Jambalaya

Serves 4

Ingredients

2 tbsp oil
2 chicken breasts, cut into pieces
8 oz (225 g) sausage (chorizo if available)
8 oz (225 g) rice
1 onion, peeled and chopped
2 cloves of garlic, peeled and finely chopped
1 green pepper, deseeded and chopped
2 sticks of celery, chopped
1 tsp cayenne pepper
1 pint (600 ml) vegetable or chicken stock
Salt
Pepper

Heat the oil in a large saucepan or a wok. Fry the onions and garlic for about five minutes, add the sausage and chicken and fry for another 5 minutes, then add the pepper and celery. Continue frying for another couple of minutes, then season and add the cayenne pepper. Pour the stock over the top and bring to the boil.

When the stock is boiling add the rice and cook for roughly 20 minutes or until the rice is soft when pinched. Be careful not to overcook the rice.

Toad in the Hole

A classic dish whose name is about as misleading as hedgehog crisps.

Serves 4

Ingredients

1 lb (500 g) sausages
1 oz (25 g) lard
4 oz (100 g) flour
1 egg
½ pint (300 ml) milk
A pinch of salt

Mix the flour and the salt, then make a well in the flour and break the egg into the well. Add first a little milk to give a smooth texture, then pour in the rest of the milk and beat for a minute or so. Put the sausages in a baking tin with the lard and bake for 10 minutes at Gas Mark 7 (450 °F, 230 °C). Then add the batter and cook for a further 25 minutes or until the batter has risen and is browned.

Spicy Sausage Casserole

This recipe is perfect for a cold winter's evening. Wash it down with a robust wine with plenty of kick.

Serves 4

Ingredients

1 pack of pork sausages, cut into pieces
1 onion, peeled and chopped
2 cloves of garlic, peeled and finely chopped
1 tin of tomatoes
2 tbsp tomato purée
1 green pepper, deseeded and chopped
1 glass of red wine
2 tsp chilli powder
1 tsp oregano
2 tbsp oil
Pepper
Salt

Heat the oil in a largish saucepan or wok, then fry the onions, garlic and chilli powder for about 5 minutes. Add the sausages and the pepper, and cook for about 10 minutes. Add the tomato purée, wine, seasoning, tomatoes and oregano. Simmer for at least 15 minutes then serve with rice and peas. Alternatively, after cooking the rice and peas add them directly to the casserole and cook for another couple of minutes. Also tastes nice with grated cheese on top.

Pasta with Sausage

It might seem like an unusual combination but it works well.

Serves 4

Ingredients

6 thick spicy sausages
14 oz (400 g) tagliatelle
1 oz (25 g) butter
Olive oil
2 oz (50 g) finely grated Parmesan
1 clove of garlic, peeled and crushed
1 courgette
2 tbsp fresh basil, finely chopped
2 tbsp fresh chives, finely chopped
2 tbsp fresh parsley, finely chopped
Salt
Pepper

Grill or fry the sausages until cooked, then cut into slices. Cook the pasta with a drop of olive oil added to the water to stop it sticking together. Cut the courgette into thin strips so that they look like matchsticks and fry in a little olive oil with the garlic for a couple of minutes. When the pasta is cooked, drain and return to the pan. Throw in the cheese, herbs, sausage and butter, mix thoroughly and season. If the cheese has not melted return to the heat for a minute.

POULTRY

Chicken Casserole

Serves 4

Ingredients

4 pieces of chicken (breast, wings or thigh)
½ pint (300 ml) chicken stock
1 tbsp tomato purée
1 onion, peeled and chopped
2 tsp flour
2 tsp oregano or mixed herbs
Salt
Pepper

Mix the flour with a little water and then combine with the chicken stock. Add the herbs, onion, tomato purée, salt and pepper. Put the chicken in an ovenproof dish, and pour the stock over it. Cover the dish with foil and bake in the oven for about 1 hour on Gas Mark 4 (180 °C, 350 °F). Serve with potatoes and vegetables.

Stuffed Chicken

If you are short of time you don't have to marinate the chicken, but you won't get the full benefit of all the flavours.

Serves 4

Ingredients

2 tbsp olive oil
4 chicken breasts
Juice of one lemon
2 cloves of garlic, peeled and finely chopped
2 tsp herbes de Provence
Boursin cheese
Pepper
Salt

Marinate the chicken breasts in the oil, lemon juice, herbs, garlic, salt and pepper for at least 4 hours. Remove the chicken from the marinade and make a split the length of the breast and stuff with the cheese. Place the chicken breast in an ovenproof dish and pour over the marinade, then sprinkle liberally with more herbes de Provence.

Place in the oven and cook for 45 minutes on Gas mark 6 (220 °C, 425 °F). Delicious served with dauphinoise potatoes and a green salad.

Spicy Chicken

Serves 4

Ingredients

2 tbsp oil
4 chicken portions, skinned
1 clove of garlic, peeled and finely chopped
2 large onions, peeled and chopped
1 tbsp paprika
¼ pint (150 ml) chicken stock
¼ pint (150 ml) soured cream
Salt
Pepper

Heat the oil in a casserole dish and fry the onions and garlic slowly for about 5 minutes. They should end up golden in colour. When cooking onions don't have the heat up too high as the onions can burn in a matter of seconds. When the onions are cooked add the chicken and paprika and continue to fry for a few minutes. Season, mix in the stock and simmer for 30 minutes.

Just before serving stir in the soured cream. Serve with rice or potatoes.

Coq au Vin

This legendary recipe is another that suits a cold winter's evening. It is traditionally made using red wine from the Burgundy region of France. Burgundy produces some of the finest wines in the world, but they come at a price, usually a high one. If you are on a budget use a robust wine from a cheaper region. It doesn't really matter where you get your coq from.

Serves 4

Ingredients

2 oz (50 g) butter
3 lb (1.5 kg) chicken, jointed
10 shallots
1 tbsp flour
8 oz (225 g) small mushrooms
4 oz (100 g) streaky bacon, chopped
1 clove of garlic, crushed
½ pint (300 ml) red wine
3 tbsp brandy
¼ pint (150 ml) chicken stock
1 bay leaf
1 tbsp fresh chopped parsley
Salt
Pepper

For the beurre manie:

2 tbsp butter
2 tbsp flour

Melt the butter in a large casserole dish, then fry the chicken pieces for 5 minutes. Remove from the dish and set aside. Fry the onions, mushrooms, garlic and bacon for 5 minutes, then add the chicken pieces. Pour over the brandy and set alight. Pour in the red wine and stock, and add the bay leaf and seasoning, then bring to the boil. Simmer for about 2 hours. Whilst the chicken is simmering prepare the beurre manie by mixing the flour and the butter together to form a soft paste. Add the beurre manie to the chicken in small pieces, stirring constantly. Remove the bay leaf before serving and garnish with the parsley.

Chicken in Wine

Serves 4

Ingredients

4 chicken pieces
1 glass of red or white wine
2 onions, peeled and chopped
½ pint (300 ml) vegetable stock
2 tbsp flour
2 tbsp oil
Pepper
Salt

Put the flour in a dish and roll the chicken pieces in it until they are evenly covered. Heat the oil in a large saucepan, then fry the onions for 5 minutes or until they are golden. Add the chicken pieces and fry for another 5 minutes. Add the stock, onions, salt, pepper and of course the wine, and simmer for 45 minutes.

Chicken Tandoori

Making your own tandoori will cost much less than buying from a takeaway or even a supermarket.

Serves 4

Ingredients

4 chicken pieces (breast, thigh or wing)
1 tbsp tandoori powder
1 clove of garlic, peeled and finely chopped
½ pint (300 ml) plain unsweetened natural yogurt

Remove the skin from the chicken and make some small incisions in the flesh with a sharp knife – this is to allow the marinade to penetrate deep into the chicken.

Mix the garlic, tandoori powder and yogurt together, then rub some of the mixture into the incisions. Leave the chicken in the marinade for at least 3 hours, turning occasionally. The longer it is left, the more flavour it will gain.

Cook under a medium grill for about 20 minutes, spooning on some more marinade at the same time. Turn the chicken over every few minutes to prevent burning.

Chicken Risotto

Risotto dishes are ideal because they are filling, cheap and easy to prepare.

Serves 4

Ingredients

1 oz (25 g) butter
1 onion, peeled and chopped
1 clove of garlic, peeled and finely chopped
6 oz (150 g) chicken, cut into pieces
8 oz (225 g) Arborio rice
2 oz (50 g) mushrooms
1 pint (600 ml)) chicken stock

Heat the butter in a large saucepan and fry the chicken pieces for 5 minutes. Remove from the pan and put in a bowl. Fry the onion and garlic for 3 to 4 minutes. Put the rice in a sieve and wash under cold water to remove the starch. Then add the rice to the onions and fry gently for a couple more minutes. Heat the stock, then add a third of it to the saucepan. After the stock has been absorbed by the rice add the rest of the stock and simmer until the rice is cooked. When the rice is cooked add the chicken and mushrooms and cook for a few minutes to heat them through.

Chicken with Garlic

This title is a bit of an understatement, perhaps it should read 'garlic with chicken'. This is one of those recipes that you might think contains a typographical error, but no, this recipe does require a large quantity of garlic. Traditionally it should use even more, but it has been scaled down a little as garlic is not particularly cheap in this country. Whole cloves are roasted alongside the chicken and when cooked, the cloves can be eaten whole. As they've been cooked for so long they lose their strong aroma, however, they take on a unique flavour that is delicious.

Serves 4

Ingredients

4 whole garlic bulbs
3 lb (1.5 kg) chicken
2 oz (50 g) butter
Juice of one lemon
Salt
Pepper

Peel half of the garlic cloves and keep the rest in their skins. Season the chicken inside and out with salt and pepper, then pour the lemon juice over the chicken, again inside and out. Stuff the peeled garlic inside with half of the butter. Smear the remaining butter over the chicken and place with the breast-side down on a baking tray. Cook in a pre-heated oven on Gas Mark 4 (350 °F, 180 °C) for 30 minutes. Remove from the oven and place the unpeeled garlic cloves around the edge of the chicken and return to the oven. After another hour, turn the chicken onto its back and cook for a further 30 minutes.

When the chicken is cooked remove from the baking tray with the garlic. Serve the chicken with the juices from the pan. The whole garlic cloves can be eaten using your fingers, or spread onto toast.

Chicken Curry with Cucumber Raita

Cucumber raita is a traditional Indian dish that is served as an accompaniment to curry. If the roof of your mouth is feeling like a furnace, this might help.

Serves 4

Ingredients

2 tbsp oil
4 chicken pieces
2 onions, peeled and chopped
2 cloves of garlic, peeled and finely chopped
3 tsp curry powder
1 tsp garam masala
2 fresh green chilli peppers, chopped into rings
1 tin of tomatoes
3 whole green cardamom pods
2 tbsp freshly chopped coriander
1 small pot of natural yogurt
1 to 2 tbsp water
Salt
Pepper

For the Cucumber Raita:

½ cucumber, peeled and chopped into pieces
1 small pot of natural yogurt
1 tbsp olive oil
1 tbsp freshly chopped mint
Pepper
Salt

To make the chicken curry, heat the oil in a large saucepan, then fry the onion and garlic gently for 5 minutes or until they have softened. Add the curry powder, garam masala and chillies, and fry for a couple more minutes. Add the chicken and water and fry for 5 minutes. After this the other ingredients can be added, apart from the yogurt, which is added 5 minutes before serving. Season to taste. Simmer for 30 to 40 minutes, then serve with rice.

To make the raita, mix the cucumber, yogurt and mint together in a bowl, pour the oil on top, and season.

Chicken in Beer

The temptation is always to leave out the chicken from this recipe, but aim for restraint.

Serves 4

Ingredients

2 tbsp oil
4 chicken pieces
1 onion, peeled and chopped
3 carrots, scraped and chopped
1 leek, sliced
4 oz (100 g) mushrooms, sliced
1 large can of your favourite lager
Salt
Pepper

Put the oil in a casserole dish, then fry the onion for 3 to 4 minutes. Add the chicken and fry for another 10 minutes. Chuck the rest of the ingredients into the dish then stick into the oven for 1 hour on Gas Mark 5 (200 °C, 400 °F).

Then drink the rest of the beer, taking care not to get so drunk that you forget to take the chicken out of the oven, or at least switch the oven off.

Lemon Chicken

This recipe is a refreshing change to the more common ways of presenting chicken.

Serves 4

Ingredients

2 tbsp olive oil
4 chicken pieces, preferably breast
Juice of 1 lemon
Pepper

Cut the chicken into small pieces (this allows the lemon to flavour a larger surface area). Heat the oil in a large frying pan, then add the chicken, lemon juice and pepper. Fry for 5 minutes or until the chicken is cooked all the way through, adding more lemon juice before serving if required.

Serve with a salad and pitta or French bread.

Chicken with Mushrooms and Peppers

Serves 4

Ingredients

2 tbsp vegetable oil
4 chicken pieces (breast, leg or thigh)
1 green pepper, deseeded and sliced into rings
4 oz (100 g) mushrooms, washed and sliced
1 pint (600 ml) chicken stock
1 onion, peeled and chopped
Salt
Pepper

Heat the oil in a medium-sized saucepan, then fry the onions and chicken for about 5 minutes. Stir in the mushrooms, peppers and seasoning and continue to fry gently for another 10 minutes. Pour the chicken stock over the top and simmer for 30 minutes. Serve with potatoes or rice.

Hot Chicken

Serves 4

Ingredients

2 tbsp oil
4 chicken pieces
1 onion, peeled and chopped
1 green pepper, deseeded and chopped
1 tin of tomatoes
2 tsp chilli powder
Salt
Pepper

Heat the oil in a large saucepan and fry the onions for 3 to 4 minutes, then add the chilli powder, salt and pepper. Cook for another couple of minutes. Add the chicken and the pepper and cook for about 10 minutes. Then mix in the tomatoes and simmer for 40 minutes, adding a little water if the sauce begins to dry out.

Serve with rice.

Roast Chicken

Ingredients

1 whole chicken
4 tbsp oil
Pepper

It is important not to overcook chicken as it loses all its flavour and is harder to carve.

Place the chicken in a baking tin, baste with the oil and season with plenty of black pepper. Cook for 15 to 20 minutes per pound plus 20 minutes on Gas Mark 6 (225 °C, 425 °F). If you want to enhance the flavour, stuff half a lemon, a spring of rosemary and a clove of garlic in the cavity.

Marinated Chicken

Serves 4

Ingredients

2 tbsp oil
4 chicken breasts
Juice of 2 lemons
2 tbsp sherry or marsala
1 tsp French mustard
Black pepper

This dish needs to be prepared a little in advance. If you don't have any sherry or marsala, it can be omitted.

Remove the skin from the chicken. Dice the chicken breasts into bite-sized pieces and put in a small mixing bowl along with the lemon juice, mustard, sherry and pepper. Mix well and leave in the fridge for several hours.

Heat the oil in a frying pan, then gently fry the chicken for about 10 minutes.

The chicken can be served with fresh vegetables of your choice and dauphinoise potatoes.

Fish

Baked Fish with Ginger

Serves 1 to 2, depending on size of fish

Ingredients

1 whole fish, such as red snapper, cleaned
1 clove of garlic, peeled and finely chopped
1 tsp soy sauce
Juice of 1 lemon
1 oz (25 g) fresh ginger, peeled and thinly sliced
Tinfoil

Place the fish on a piece of foil. Mix the lemon juice, soy sauce, garlic and ginger together and pour over the fish. Seal the fish in the foil and bake in the oven for 45 minutes at Gas Mark 5 (200 °C, 400 °F).

Halibut Casserole

Serves 4

Ingredients

2 tbsp oil
4 halibut steaks
1 onion, peeled and chopped
½ pint (300 ml) white wine
1 garlic clove, peeled and crushed
1 tbsp cornflour
8 oz (225 g) tomatoes, skinned, deseeded and
chopped
1 tbsp tomato purée
Salt
Pepper

Heat the oil in a casserole dish. Add the onion and garlic and fry gently for 3 to 4 minutes. Stir in the cornflour, tomatoes, tomato purée and the wine. Bring slowly to the boil, stirring constantly, then add the fish and simmer for 10 minutes or until the fish is cooked. The perfect accompaniment is mashed potato.

Grilled Cod

Serves 1

Ingredients

1 cod steak
Butter
Pepper
Salt

Pre-heat the grill to its hottest setting. Brush the fish with a little butter, season and grill for about 10 minutes, according to the size and thickness of the fish. Turn occasionally.

If you like a bit more flavour, squeeze some lemon or lime juice on top. Serve with potatoes or rice, and fresh vegetables.

Baked Fish in Wine

Serves 2

Ingredients

2 cod steaks
1 onion, peeled and cut into rings
1 glass of wine, red or white
Pepper
Salt

Put the fish and onions in a shallow baking dish, season and pour the wine over the top. Bake in the oven for 35 minutes at Gas Mark 5 (200 °C, 400 °F).

Kedgeree

Serves 4

Ingredients

1 egg
8 oz (225 g) rice
8 oz (225 g) smoked haddock fillet
2 oz (50 g) butter
Juice of 1 lemon
Milk
Pepper
Salt

Place the haddock in a shallow frying pan and cover with milk. Cook gently over a low heat for about 10 minutes. Then remove from the oven and flake the fish with a fork, removing all bones and skin. Cook the rice according to the instructions on the packet.

Rinse the rice cooked in boiling water – this gets rid of most of the starch. Hard boil the egg by boiling it for 10 minutes. Then cool, remove the shell and chop into pieces.

Melt the butter in a saucepan and add the fish. Cook the fish for 3 to 4 minutes to reheat it. Stir in the lemon juice, chopped egg, seasoning and rice and serve immediately. Garnish with fresh parsley.

Fish Cakes

Serves 4

Ingredients

8 oz (225 g) cooked cod
8 oz (225 g) mashed potato
1 oz (25 g) melted butter
1 egg, beaten
Dried breadcrumbs
1 tbsp chopped parsley
1 tsp capers
Salt
Pepper

Remove the skin and bones from the fish and flake. Mix the fish, potato, parsley, capers, butter, salt and pepper together. Shape into 6 to 8 cakes by hand. Dip the fish cakes into the egg mixture, then roll in the breadcrumbs. Shallow fry in hot fat until they are golden-brown on both sides.

Baked Trout

Serves 2

Ingredients

2 small trout, cleaned
1 onion, peeled and finely chopped
1 carrot, peeled and finely chopped
1 clove of garlic, peeled and finely chopped
1 oz (25 g) flaked almonds
½ oz (15 g) butter
Salt
Pepper

Melt the butter in a frying pan, then add the onion, carrot, and garlic. Fry for about 5 minutes. Place each trout on a piece of tinfoil, making sure the foil is big enough to completely wrap the fish. Divide the vegetables between the two fish, placing the vegetables on the top and the sides of the fish. Sprinkle with the almonds, season, then seal up the tinfoil parcels.

Bake in the oven for about 20 minutes on Gas Mark 5 (200 °C, 400 °F).

Serve with potatoes, rice or salad.

Grilled Sardines

Fresh sardines are a favourite in France. In June, they have special parties to celebrate this little fish called Sardinières. The sardines are served grilled with plenty of salt and lemon. If the sardines are small enough they are not normally gutted, but if they are large then have the fishmonger gut them for you as this is a fiddly process.

Serves 4

Ingredients

16 small sardines
Olive oil
Salt
Lemon

Pre-heat the grill to its hottest setting, then place the sardines on the grill pan. Brush with a little oil, sprinkle with salt and cook for 4 minutes on each side. They taste even better if they are barbecued. Serve with lemon juice and a simple salad, bread and wine.

Cod and Onion Bake

Serves 4

Ingredients

4 pieces of cod or any white fish
1 large onion, peeled and sliced into separate rings
3 sliced tomatoes
2 tsp capers
2 oz (50 g) butter

This is an easy dish to prepare that should take no more than 5 minutes. Put the fish and onion into an ovenproof dish with the butter, and bake for 20 minutes on Gas Mark 5 (200 °C, 400 °F). Add the sliced tomatoes and capers and cook for a further 10 minutes.

Serve with potatoes and fresh vegetables.

Tomato and Tuna Pasta Sauce

Serves 4

Ingredients

2 tbsp olive oil
1 medium onion, peeled and chopped
1 clove of garlic, peeled and finely chopped
1 tbsp fresh rosemary, finely chopped
1 tin of tomatoes
1 tbsp tomato purée
1 tin of tuna
1 tsp brown sugar
Salt
Pepper

Heat the oil in a medium-sized saucepan and fry the onions and garlic for about 5 minutes. Add the tomatoes, purée, rosemary, salt, pepper, sugar. Simmer for about 15 minutes or until the sauce has been reduced, then add the tuna and simmer for a further 5 minutes.

Serve with a pasta of your choice and sprinkle with Parmesan.

Vegetarian Dishes

Over the past decade the interest in vegetarian food has escalated. Whatever the reason for becoming a vegetarian it is a misconception that vegetarian cooking is boring. The people that say this are the sort of people that eat pie and chips every night and think that a courgette is some sort of American car. I am certainly not a vegetarian, but enjoy vegetarian food. There is great scope for experimentation with vegetables. Try to get away from the meat and two veg mentality, be bold, and you might be pleasantly surprised.

Piperade

This is one of those dishes that is quick and easy to prepare and is suitable for a light lunch or supper. The dish originates from the Basque country. Add a pinch of paprika if you want it with a little bite.

Serves 4

Ingredients

6 eggs
2 tbsp butter
2 red peppers, deseeded
2 green peppers, deseeded
2 cloves of garlic, peeled and chopped
6 tomatoes, skinned
1 tbsp chopped fresh basil
Salt
Pepper

Cut the peppers into strips and chop the tomatoes. Heat the butter in a frying pan and cook the peppers for 10 minutes. Add the chopped tomatoes, garlic, basil and seasoning and cook until the tomatoes are almost a pulp. Take care that the vegetables do not burn. Whilst the vegetables are cooking, beat the eggs in a basin. When the vegetables are ready add the eggs. Stir the mixture until it thickens, but do not let the eggs set completely. This dish is traditionally served with slices of fried ham.

Aubergine Bake

Serves 4

Ingredients

2 tbsp oil
1 large aubergine, thinly sliced
2 onions, peeled and chopped
2 cloves of garlic, chopped
5 oz (125 g) pot of natural yogurt
1 tin of tomatoes
1 tbsp tomato purée
1 tsp dried oregano
3 oz (75 g) grated cheddar cheese
1 oz (25 g) white breadcrumbs
Salt
Pepper

Heat the oil in a frying pan. Cook the aubergine in stages. Fry the aubergine until it has softened and slightly browned, then place on kitchen paper to absorb the oil. After cooking all the aubergine, remove it and fry the onion and garlic for 5 minutes.

The next stage is to add the tomato, tomato purée, oregano and seasoning. Bring to the boil, then simmer for 10 minutes before stirring in the yogurt.

Using a greased ovenproof dish, arrange the aubergine then the tomato sauce in alternate layers. Continue this until the top layer is of aubergine. Cover the top with breadcrumbs and cheese.

Bake at Gas Mark 4 (180 °C, 350 °F), for 30 minutes. Serve with rice or potatoes.

Jacket Potato

It is important to use old potatoes – new ones are not suitable. This also applies to roast potatoes.

Serves 1

Ingredients

1 large potato

After viciously stabbing your potato with a sharp implement (preferably a fork), bung in the oven for about 60 minutes on Gas Mark 7 (230 °C, 450 °F).

Test the potato with a skewer or a knife to see if it is cooked in the middle. The skewer should pass easily through the potato.

Jacket Potato with Cheese and Onion

This is another way of cooking jacket potatoes, but it takes a little more time to prepare and to eat.

Serves 1

Ingredients

1 large potato
2 oz (50 g) cheddar cheese, grated
1 onion
1 tbsp milk
A knob of butter

Follow the instructions for the above recipe. Slice the cooked potato in half. Scoop the potato out of the skin using a teaspoon and place the contents into a mixing bowl. Try not to make a hole in the skins because you'll need them later.

Add the milk and butter and mash. Cut the onion up into pieces and fry for 3 to 4 minutes. Add the onion to the potato and mix together. Then spoon the potato back into the jackets, cover with cheese and cook in the oven for another 15 minutes or so. If the cheese starts to burn cover the potato with a piece of tinfoil.

Macaroni Cheese

This is another of my favourite recipes. If you don't have any macaroni use pasta shells.

Serves 4

Ingredients

6 oz (150 g) macaroni
6 oz (150 g) grated cheddar cheese
2 large tomatoes
¾ pint (450 ml) milk
1 oz (25 g) flour or cornflour
1 oz (25 g) butter

Melt the butter in a saucepan and mix in the flour. Gradually add the milk, stirring constantly to prevent lumps. Bring to the boil, add the cheese, then leave to simmer for 3 to 4 minutes.

Now cook the macaroni according to the instructions on the packet. When this is done, drain and mix with the cheese sauce. Put into a baking dish, top with sliced tomatoes and more cheese. Grill until browned.

Cabbage Parcels

Serves 2

Ingredients

6 large cabbage leaves
8 oz (225 g) spinach
6 oz (150 g) cooked rice
2 oz (50 g) butter
4 oz (100 g) grated cheddar cheese
1 egg yolk
½ pint (300 ml) vegetable stock

First, simmer the spinach in a little water for 5 minutes, then drain and put aside. Simmer the cabbage leaves for about two minutes and remove from the water.

Melt the butter and add the chopped onion together with the rice, spinach, cheese, and seasoning. Bind with the egg yolk.

When thoroughly mixed, put a heaped spoonful of it onto each of the cabbage leaves, and wrap into parcels. Place the parcels in an ovenproof dish and pour the stock on top.

Cover with foil and bake for 30 minutes at Gas Mark 4 (180 °C, 350 °F).

Potato and Tomato Cake

Serves 4

Ingredients

2 tbsp oil
2 lb (1 kg) 'old' potatoes
1 tin of tomatoes
1 onion, peeled and finely chopped
Salt
Pepper

Heat the oil in a pan and fry the onion gently for 10 minutes, then add the tomatoes, salt and pepper. Keep the heat low and simmer for about 20 minutes so the sauce reduces to a thick liquid. Whilst the sauce is reducing boil the potatoes until they are soft enough to mash. When they get to this stage mash them. Gradually mix the sauce with the mashed potatoes. When all the sauce is added, spoon the mixture out onto a serving plate and mould into the shape of a cake. Eat hot or cold.

Vegetable Stir-Fry

Those fortunate enough to possess a wok will find Oriental cooking a lot easier than those stuck with the indignity of a frying pan. If you do have to use a frying pan, use the biggest one you have. The wok is one of my most used kitchen accessories. Its use does not have to be confined to Oriental cooking.

It is up to you what to put into a stir-fry, though it is often a good way of using up any spare vegetables that are lurking at the back of your cupboard. Experiment with exotic vegetables, oils and pastes.

Serves 4

Ingredients

2 tbsp oil
1 onion, peeled and chopped
1 red pepper, deseeded and chopped
1 green pepper, deseeded and chopped
1 carrot, cut into thin strips
1 clove of garlic, peeled and finely chopped
1 tin of bamboo shoots
1 tin of water chestnuts
1 pack of fresh bean sprouts
2 tbsp soy sauce
Salt
Pepper

Pour the oil into your wok, then when the oil is hot, add the onion and garlic, and fry for 5 minutes. If you are using water chestnuts, cook these first as they take the longest to cook, and are nicer when they are slightly crispy. Add the soy sauce, seasoning, and other vegetables except for the beansprouts.

After frying the vegetables for 5 to 10 minutes, add the beansprouts and cook for a couple more minutes. It is important to keep the beansprouts firm. Serve with rice.

Lentil Curry

Serves 2

Ingredients

2 tbsp oil
4 oz (100 g) lentils, soaked in cold water for 1 hour
½ pint (300 ml) vegetable stock
4 carrots, scraped and chopped
1 onion, peeled and chopped
1 courgette, sliced
1 leek, sliced
1 tbsp curry powder
2 fresh tomatoes, sliced
Salt
Pepper

Boil the lentils for about 7 minutes and then strain. Heat the oil in a large saucepan, then fry the onions and curry powder for 5 minutes. Add the other vegetables and fry for another 5 minutes. Then pour in the stock and lentils, bring to the boil, and simmer for an hour. Season.

Ratatouille

Serves 4

Ingredients

2 tbsp oil
1 tin of tomatoes
1 onion, peeled and finely chopped
2 cloves of garlic, peeled and finely chopped
1 small aubergine, chopped
1 red pepper, deseeded and chopped
1 courgette, sliced
1 lemon, quartered
2 tsp herbes de Provence
1 bay leaves
1 glass of red wine, water or tomato juice (optional)
Pepper
Salt

While you are preparing the other vegetables, place the pieces of aubergine on a plate and sprinkle them with salt.

After preparing the other vegetables, wash the aubergine pieces, then dry them with kitchen paper.

Heat the oil in a large saucepan. Fry the onions and garlic for about 5 minutes, then add the courgette, the aubergines and the peppers. Cook for about 5 minutes before adding the tomatoes, lemon, and other ingredients. Bring to the boil and simmer for 30 minutes.

Fruit and Nut Pasta

The pine nuts and the sultanas are an unusual combination but you will find the pasta delicious.

Serves 4

Ingredients

8 tbsp olive oil
14 oz (400 g) pasta
2 cloves of garlic, peeled and finely chopped
2 oz (50 g) sultanas
2 oz (50 g) pine nuts
Pepper

Cook the pasta of your choice according to the instructions on the packet.

Drain the pasta and place in a serving bowl. Pour the oil over the pasta then stir in the garlic, pine nuts and sultanas. Season using lots of fresh ground pepper and serve immediately. Parmesan can be added on top if required.

Crunchy Rice

Serves 2 to 4

Ingredients

2 tbsp oil
2 cups of brown rice
4 cups of water
1 green pepper, deseeded and chopped
1 small tin of sweetcorn
1 onion, peeled and chopped
1 oz (25 g) mushrooms, sliced
1 clove of garlic, peeled and finely chopped
2 oz (50 g) walnuts
1 vegetarian Oxo cube
1 tbsp fresh chopped parsley
Salt
Pepper

Heat the oil in a large frying pan or wok, then fry the onions and garlic for between 4 and 5 minutes. Add the mushrooms, green pepper and sweetcorn and fry for another couple of minutes. Next add the uncooked rice and about four cups of water. Sprinkle the Oxo cube over and stir frequently. Simmer for about 20 minutes, depending on the type of rice used. Add more water if necessary to stop the rice from drying out.

If the rice is soft when pinched then it is cooked. Add the walnuts a couple of minutes before removing from the heat. Season with salt and pepper and garnish with the parsley.

Vegetarian Lasagne

You can use tofu, a meat substitute, with this recipe. It sounds like a Greek island, but it tastes a bit better than that. If you can find some, prepare in the same way as the meat lasagne, substituting the meat for tofu.

Serves 4

Ingredients

2 tbsp oil
1 large onion, peeled and chopped
1 red pepper, deseeded and chopped
1 green pepper, deseeded and chopped
1 clove of garlic, peeled and finely chopped
1 leek, finely chopped
2 courgettes, finely sliced
1 tin of tomatoes
2 tbsp tomato purée
2 tsp oregano
1 packet of lasagne ('no pre-cooking required' type)
Salt
Pepper

For the cheese sauce:

1 oz (25 g) butter
2 oz (50 g) flour
1 pint (600 ml) milk
6 oz (150 g) cheese, grated

Heat the oil in a large saucepan and add the onion and garlic. Cook for 5 minutes, then stir in the leek, peppers and courgette. Fry gently for another 3 minutes or so. Add the tomatoes, purée, oregano and seasoning. Bring to the boil then simmer for a further 20 minutes. While the vegetable sauce is simmering prepare the cheese sauce.

Melt the butter in a saucepan and add the flour, stirring constantly. Remove from the heat and add the milk in stages. Then bring to the boil and add the cheese, saving a bit for the top. Simmer for 3 or 4 minutes. Add more flour if the sauce refuses to thicken.

Grease a shallow baking dish, then add a layer of tomato sauce, a layer of lasagne, a layer of cheese sauce, a layer of lasagne, and so on, making sure to end up with cheese sauce on top. Sprinkle the reserved cheese on top.

Bake in a pre-heated oven for around 25 minutes at Gas Mark 6 (220 °C, 425 °F).

Hot Vegetable Stew

Serves 4

Ingredients

2 tbsp oil
1 onion, peeled and chopped
2 cloves of garlic, peeled and finely chopped
1 pepper, deseeded and sliced
2 courgettes, sliced
1 leek, sliced
1 tin of tomatoes
3 potatoes, peeled and diced
Small can of sweetcorn
4 oz (100 g) cooked green lentils
1 green chilli pepper, chopped
Dash of Tabasco sauce
1 pint (600 ml) vegetable stock
2 tsp mixed herbs
Salt
Pepper

Heat the oil in a large casserole dish, then fry the onions and garlic adding the chilli and Tabasco, for 3 to 4 minutes. Add the courgettes, leeks and peppers and gently fry for a further 10 minutes. Then add the stock and the remaining ingredients. Bring to the boil and simmer for 30 minutes.

Stuffed Peppers

Serves 4

Ingredients

2 tbsp olive oil
4 peppers
1 onion, peeled and chopped
1 clove of garlic, peeled and finely chopped
1 tin of tomatoes
2 tsp tomato purée
4 oz (100 g) mushrooms
1 glass of red wine
1 tbsp chopped parsley
1 tsp chopped rosemary
Dash of lemon juice
2 tbsp breadcrumbs
Salt
Pepper

Cut the tops off the peppers and remove the seeds, then place in boiling water for 3 to 4 minutes. Remove and plunge in cold water.

Heat the oil in a large saucepan, then gently fry the onion and garlic for a few minutes. Add the other ingredients, bring to the boil and then simmer for 10 minutes. Fill the peppers with the mixture, replace the lid of the pepper and bake in a pre-heated oven for 35 minutes on Gas Mark 6 (220 °C, 425 °F).

French Beans with Garlic

If you have runner beans they can be used instead.

Serves 4

Ingredients

1 lb (500 g) French beans
1 clove of garlic, peeled and finely chopped
1 oz (25 g) butter
Salt
Pepper

Top and tail the beans, then cut in two. Place the beans in a pan of salted boiling water and cook for 10 minutes or until tender. It is important that they are not overcooked as they will lose their colour and flavour. When cooked, drain the beans. Heat the butter in the pan and let it melt, but don't let it burn. Add the garlic and cook for a minute, then add the beans and season. Stir the beans to make sure they are evenly coated before serving.

Courgettes can be cooked in a similar way, except they do not need to be boiled, they can be fried gently in the butter with the garlic.

Dauphinoise Potatoes

If I could only eat potatoes cooked one way it would have to be this. The combination of potatoes and cream is delicious. They go particularly well with dishes such as hot vegetable stew or chicken in beer.

Serves 4

Ingredients

2 lb (1 kg) 'old' potatoes, peeled and thinly sliced
1 large onion, peeled and thinly sliced
2 cloves of garlic, peeled and crushed
½ pint (300 ml) double cream
2 oz (50 g) butter
Nutmeg
Salt
Pepper

Grease the base and sides of an ovenproof dish, then put alternate layers of onion, potato, garlic, slices of butter, cream, salt, pepper and grated nutmeg in the dish. Only use a small amount of nutmeg on each layer, otherwise the flavour may be overpowering. Finish with a layer of potatoes. Place in a pre-heated oven at Gas Mark 5 (200 °C, 400 °F) for 90 minutes. If required, freshly grated cheese such as Gruyère or Parmesan can be added.

Tomato Pasta Sauce

This is the basis of many pasta sauces, so master this before you try anything complicated. Try and use fresh Parmesan that has not been grated.

Serves 3 to 4

Ingredients

2 tbsp olive oil
1 large onion, peeled and chopped
2 cloves of garlic, peeled and finely chopped
1 tin of tomatoes
1 tbsp tomato purée
2 oz (50 g) Parmesan cheese
6 fresh basil leaves, roughly torn, or 1 tsp dried
oregano
Salt
Pepper

Heat the oil in a saucepan, then add the chopped onion and garlic and fry gently for 3 to 4 minutes or until the onions have turned almost translucent. When these have softened, add the tomatoes, purée, herbs, salt and pepper. Cook for another 20 minutes until the sauce is reduced, then add the cheese.

Serve with a pasta of your choice.

Poor Man's Pasta

There are few recipes that are this simple yet taste this good. A perfect dish to repel a hunger attack, and it only takes a few minutes to prepare.

Serves 1

Ingredients

4 oz (100 g) any pasta
½ clove of garlic, finely chopped
2 tbsp olive oil
Salt
Pepper

Cook the pasta according to the instructions on the packet. When the pasta is cooked, drain and place in a small serving bowl. Add the oil and garlic, then season with plenty of black pepper. If you wish to make it a little more exciting add a dash of Tabasco sauce or chilli pepper.

Vegetable Kebabs

Although meat is the preferred choice for cooking on a barbecue, vegetarians and pigs would probably disagree.

Serves 4

Ingredients

Olive oil
1 onion, peeled
1 red pepper, deseeded
1 yellow pepper, deseeded
4 tomatoes
1 courgette
12 mushrooms
Mixed herbs
Salt
Pepper

It really depends on the size of your skewers as to how many vegetables you use.

Prepare the vegetables by cutting them into chunks, then thread the vegetables onto the skewers, alternating between the different vegetables.

Coat the kebabs with olive oil and mixed herbs, and place on the barbecue or under a medium grill. When cooking the kebabs they need to be turned frequently to stop them burning. Season and serve with a salad.

Pesto

This recipe uses insane quantities of fresh basil, but the aroma is intoxicating. Pesto is traditionally served with pasta, but it can be spread on toast. It can be made in larger quantities and kept in a screw-top jar in the fridge.

Serves 4

Ingredients

2 cloves of garlic, peeled and crushed
2 oz (50 g) pine nuts
2 cups fresh basil leaves
3 tbsp finely grated fresh Parmesan
¼ pint (150 ml) olive oil
Salt

Put the basil leaves, pine nuts and the garlic in a blender and grind for a few seconds. Then add the cheese, oil and salt and mix well. If you are a stickler for authenticity, then you should prepare the pesto in a mortar, but a blender is far quicker. Serve with the pasta of your choice.

Supper and Snacks

There are certain times when you will not be in the mood for cooking an elaborate meal or you might just fancy something light and quick and easy to prepare. It is often the case of seeing what ingredients you have and creating a recipe from what is available.

Ham and Eggs

This is a perfect supper dish that takes only a few minutes to prepare.

Serves 4

Ingredients

4 large eggs
4 slices of ham
1 tin of chopped tomatoes
Herbes de Provence
Salt
Pepper

Heat the oven to its maximum temperature. Pour the tomatoes into a baking dish then roll up the slices of ham and place on top of the tomatoes. Break the eggs carefully on top of the ham, sprinkle with the herbs and season. Bake until the eggs are cooked. Serve with hot buttered toast.

B.L.T.

Otherwise known as a bacon, lettuce and tomato sandwich.

Serves 1

Ingredients

Butter
3 slices of bread
2 rashers of bacon
A lettuce leaf or two
1 tomato
Salt
Pepper

Remove the crusts from the bread, then slice the tomato. Grill the bacon and the bread. Butter the toast, then place a bit of lettuce, some tomato and a rasher of bacon on it. Put a slice of toast on top and then make up another layer as before. Finish with the last piece of toast on top, then cut diagonally across. Add a dash of salt and pepper if required.

To stop the B.L.T. from falling apart you could try skewering it with a cocktail stick, but under no circumstances should you swallow the cocktail stick in your haste to eat your masterpiece – they are not particularly palatable.

Egg Hubble-Bubble

Serves 1 to 2

Ingredients

4 potatoes, boiled
Any other vegetables
Butter or margarine
Cheese
4 eggs, lightly beaten and seasoned

Dice the potato, then fry it with any other vegetables you may have (for example, mushrooms, tomatoes, peas) in butter or margarine. When cooked, pour in the eggs and sprinkle with grated cheese. Cook very slowly with a plate or lid over the top until the eggs are set.

Mini Roast Potatoes with Bacon

Serves 4

Ingredients

2 lb (1 kg) 'old' potatoes
6 rashers of bacon
Herbes de Provence
Olive oil
Salt
Pepper

Peel the potatoes and cut into one-inch cubes. Cut the bacon into small pieces. Place the potatoes in a large baking tin with the bacon, sprinkle with herbs and then season. Baste with oil so that all the potatoes are evenly coated.

Place in a pre-heated oven on Gas Mark 6 (225 °C, 425 °F) and cook until crisp. This should take about 50-60 minutes.

Quiche Lorraine

The most famous quiche of all has to be the Lorraine. Its name derives from its region of origin, and it is delicious eaten hot or cold. For this recipe an 8-inch (20 cm) flan dish and a rolling pin are needed.

Serves 4

Ingredients

For the pastry case:

8 oz (225 g) plain flour
4 oz (100g) margarine or butter
2/3 tbsp water
A pinch of salt

For the filling:

4 eggs
½ pint (300 ml) double cream
4 rashers of bacon
2 oz (50 g) cheese (optional)
Salt
Pepper

To make the pastry case, sieve the flour and the salt. Cut the margarine or butter into little cubes, then rub into the flour. 'Rubbing in' is when you use your fingertips to combine the flour and the fat until the mixture has the consistency of fine breadcrumbs.

After rubbing in, add some water a little at a time. The water is needed to bind the mixture together, but be careful not to add so much that the pastry becomes sticky. Mould the pastry into a ball then roll out on a floured board or a very clean floured work surface. Also sprinkle a coating of flour onto the rolling pin. The flour is used to stop the pastry from sticking to the board and the pin.

Roll the pastry so that its area is big enough to cover the flan dish, then carefully place the pastry over the dish and mould it in the shape of the dish. Remove the edge of the overlapping pastry by running a knife around the rim of dish.

Prick the base with a fork twice then place in the fridge for 30 minutes. After removing the case from the fridge it needs to be pre-cooked in the oven before the filling is added.

Bake in the oven on Gas Mark 6 (225 °C, 425 °F) for 10 minutes.

To make the filling, cut the bacon into small pieces, then fry lightly for a couple of minutes and place on the bottom of the pastry case. Beat the eggs together, add the cream, season and beat again. Pour over the bacon, sprinkle the cheese on top if required and bake in a hot oven on Gas Mark 6 (220 °C, 425 °F), for 25 minutes or until the filling has set.

Cheese and Onion Quiche

Serves 4

Ingredients

1 pastry case (see previous recipe)
1 tbsp oil
4 eggs
½ pint (300 ml) milk
4 oz (100 g) grated cheddar cheese
1 onion, peeled and chopped
Salt
Pepper

Lightly fry the onions in the oil for a couple of minutes. Place the onion on the bottom of the pastry case. Beat the eggs together, add the milk, season and beat again. Pour over the onion, sprinkle the cheese on top, then bake in a hot oven on Gas Mark 6 (220 °C, 425 °F) for 25 minutes or until the filling is cooked.

Nachos

This is a quick and easy recipe that is perfect for any occasion.

Serves 4

Ingredients

2 tbsp oil
2 cloves of garlic, peeled and finely chopped
2 tsp chilli powder
1 large onion, peeled and chopped
1 tin of chopped tomatoes
1 large bag of tortilla chips
4 oz (100 g) grated cheese
1 tbsp tomato purée
1 green pepper, deseeded and finely chopped
Salt
Pepper

Heat the oil in a large saucepan, then fry the onion and garlic for 3 to 4 minutes. Add the chilli powder and the green pepper and cook for another couple of minutes. Then add the tomatoes, tomato purée and seasoning and cook for about 15 minutes. The sauce has to be well reduced otherwise it will make the chips soggy.

Whilst the sauce is cooking arrange the tortilla chips in a ceramic dish. When the sauce is ready, pour over the chips and finally cover with cheese. Then place under a hot grill until the cheese has melted. Enjoy.

Spanish Omelette

As there are numerous variations on this meal, don't hold yourself back with what you add.

Serves 4

Ingredients

4 eggs
1 potato, cooked for 10 minutes and chopped
2 tomatoes, sliced
1 oz (25 g) peas
1 onion, peeled and chopped
Mixed herbs
Salt
Pepper

Beat the eggs, season, add the vegetables and pour into a flan dish. Bake at Gas Mark 6 (220 °C, 425 °F) for 15 to 20 minutes or until the mixture ceases to be runny. If you prefer the onions to be a little more cooked, fry them first for a few minutes.

Serve with a green salad.

Welsh Rarebit

Doesn't taste particularly Welsh, nor is it very rare.

Serves 1

Ingredients

6 oz (150 g) cheddar cheese
½ oz (15 g) butter
½ tsp dry mustard
2 tbsp flour
2 slices of bread
4 rashers of streaky bacon

Grate the cheese and put into a small saucepan. Add the butter and mustard, then cook gently, stirring constantly, until the cheese has melted. Take the saucepan away from the heat and add the flour, beating it in until smooth. Allow to cool.

Grill the bacon and the bread, then spread the cheese mixture evenly over the toast. Grill until golden, then add the bacon and serve.

Pan Bagnat

Serves 1

Ingredients

1 very large roll
1 tbsp olive oil
Wine vinegar
Sliced tomato
Tuna
Sliced egg
1 clove of garlic
Sliced cucumber
3 black olives
2 slices of green pepper
Salt
Pepper

Cut the roll in half and tear out some of the centre of the roll to allow room for the filling. Take the clove of garlic and cut in half then rub the inside of the roll with the cut edge. Pour a tablespoon of the oil over the inside of the roll. Fill the roll with the rest of the ingredients, pour the remaining oil evenly over, sprinkle with a few drops of vinegar, season and put the top back on. Press down on the top of the roll with a degree of force to combine the flavours together. Do not serve immediately as it is best to wait a little while for the oil to penetrate the roll.

Best eaten sitting on the beach, with a cold beer.

Plain Omelette

Serves 1 to 2

Ingredients

1 oz (25 g) butter
2 or 3 eggs
A pinch of mixed herbs
Salt
Pepper

Beat the eggs together in a mixing bowl and add the seasoning. Melt the butter in a frying pan and pour in the eggs. As soon as the eggs start to cook lift up one edge of the omelette with a spatula, tilt the pan and let the uncooked egg run underneath. Continue to do this until the omelette is cooked, then flip it in half and serve on a warmed plate.

Cheese and Tomato Omelette

Serves 1 to 2

Ingredients

1 oz (25 g) butter
2 or 3 eggs
2 oz (50 g) grated cheese
1 chopped tomato
Salt
Pepper

Beat the eggs together in a mixing bowl and add the seasoning, cheese and tomato. Melt the butter in a frying pan and pour in the eggs. As soon as the eggs start to cook lift up one edge of the omelette with a spatula, tilt the pan and let the uncooked egg run underneath. Continue to do this until the omelette is cooked, then flip it in half and serve on a warmed plate.

Eggy Bread

Serves 2

Ingredients

3 eggs
4 tbsp milk
Slices of bread without the crusts
2 tbsp oil
Pepper

Beat the eggs and the milk together and season. Heat the oil in a frying pan. Dip a slice of bread in the egg mixture and then fry for a couple of minutes on each side.

Egg and Cheese Ramekins

Serves 1

Ingredients

2 oz (50 g) grated cheese
1 egg
1 tomato
Salt
Pepper

Grease a small ovenproof dish, preferably a ramekin dish or one that is about 3 inches (7.5 cm) in diameter. Put grated cheese in the bottom of the dish and up the sides. Place in a slice of tomato and then the egg, trying not to break the yolk. Add the seasoning and cover with another slice of tomato and more grated cheese.

Bake in the oven for about 15 minutes at Gas Mark 4 (180 °C, 350 °F) or until the eggs are set.

Scrambled Egg

Serves 2

Ingredients

3 eggs
1 oz (25 g) butter
4 tbsp milk
Pepper

Beat the eggs in a bowl and add the milk and pepper. Melt the butter in a saucepan and add the egg mixture. Stir the mixture as it thickens. Don't have the heat up too high, or else the egg will burn and stick to the pan.

Serve on top of hot buttered toast.

Poached Egg

Ingredients

1 egg
Butter

Put a knob of butter in one of the poacher rings, when melted add the egg and cook for about 4 minutes, according to taste.

There is a more traditional way of poaching eggs: boil some water in a saucepan. When the water is boiling stir the water with a spoon and the having broken an egg into a cup or mug slide it into the water. Cook gently for 4 minutes. Remove the egg with a slotted spoon and drain on kitchen towel. Serve on hot buttered toast.

Fried Egg

Ingredients

1 egg
2 tbsp oil

Put the oil in a non-stick frying pan. Don't let the fat get too hot, otherwise the egg will stick to the pan and bubble. Crack the egg on the side of the pan and plop the egg into the oil. Fry gently for about 3 minutes, basting occasionally. If you like your eggs American style (sunny-side down), fry both sides of the egg.

Desserts

As a child it was the desserts that proved to be my weakness. Anything with obscene amounts of chocolate and cream was shovelled down in amazing quantities. Those days of carefree eating are now over as that unfortunate phenomenon when you stop growing taller and instead grow outwards has taken over.

Fresh Fruit Salad

Not even a hint of chocolate.

Serves 4

Ingredients

1 banana
2 oranges
1 apple
1 pear
2 oz (50 g) grapes
4 oz (100 g) strawberries
Juice of 1 lemon
2 tbsp sugar
½ pint (150 ml) water

The above ingredients are just a guide. You can use any fruit that is available or affordable.

Wash all fruit before starting. Put the lemon juice and sugar in a mixing bowl and mix together.

Cut the apple into quarters, remove the core and chop into small pieces.

Peel the oranges using a sharp knife, making sure all the pips are removed. Cut into segments, cutting between the membranes.

Cut the grapes in half and remove the pips. Peel the banana and cut into slices.

Skin and quarter the pear, then core it and chop into small pieces. The strawberries should be hulled (that means remove the green bit at the top), and cut in half.

Put all the fruit in the bowl with the lemon juice, sugar, and water, and mix thoroughly.

Serve either on its own or with cream.

Pears in Red Wine

Serves 4

Ingredients

4 pears
4 oz (100 g) sugar
¼ pint (150 ml) red wine
¼ pint (150 ml) water
Pinch of cinnamon
1 oz (25 g) browned almond flakes

Put the wine, water, sugar and cinnamon in a large saucepan and heat gently until the sugar has dissolved. Peel the pears, trying not to damage the fruit, and leave the stalks on. Place the pears in the wine and simmer for about 20 minutes or until they are soft. When the pears are cooked remove from the pan and place in a serving dish. Reduce the wine sauce by boiling rapidly. It should become syrupy. Pour the wine over the pears and when cool, chill in the fridge. Before serving sprinkle with almonds and serve with cream.

Ricotta and Raspberry Crunch

A delicious summer pudding that does not have to be made with raspberries. You could use strawberries, bananas or grapes instead. Another variation uses toasted pine nuts instead of the almonds.

Serves 4

Ingredients

12 oz (300 g) ricotta cheese
8 oz (225 g) fresh raspberries
Toasted almonds
Runny honey

Divide the ricotta into four bowls and arrange the raspberries around the edge of the cheese. Put about a tablespoon of honey on top of the cheese and then sprinkle with the toasted almonds. If you find that it is a little bitter, either add more honey or dust with caster sugar.

Baked Apples

Ingredients

1 large cooking apple per person
Mincemeat
Brown sugar
Butter

Remove the cores from the apples and stand them in an ovenproof dish. Fill the hole in the apple with mincemeat and a teaspoon of brown sugar. Add a knob of butter on top. Put enough water in the dish to cover the bottom of the apples. Bake at Gas Mark 4 (180 °C, 350 °F) for about an hour.

After an hour test the apple with a skewer. It should be soft, but not mushy. Serve with cream or ice cream.

Raspberry Brulée

Serves 4

Ingredients

**8 oz (225 g) fresh raspberries
½ pint (300 ml) double cream or whipping cream
6 oz (150 g) demerara or golden granulated sugar**

Place the raspberries in a shallow heatproof dish. Whip the cream until thick (but not too stiff) and spread over the raspberries. Sprinkle the sugar over the cream, covering it completely.

Pre-heat the grill and then place the brulée under the grill until it is dark and bubbling. Remove from the grill and cool. Chill in the fridge for a couple of hours. A cheaper version could be made using sliced banana.

Poached Peaches

Serves 4

Ingredients

1 tin of peach halves
½ oz (15 g) butter or margarine
2 tbsp brown or golden granulated sugar
1 tbsp brandy or whisky (optional)

Drain the syrup from the peaches, reserving a small amount. Melt the butter in a saucepan. Add the peaches with the syrup and sugar. Heat gently for about 5 minutes then stir in the brandy.

If you have any flaked almonds or nuts, a few of these toasted and sprinkled on top taste good.

Croissant Pudding

Serves 4

Ingredients

5 croissants
½ pint (300 ml) milk
2 oz (50 g) castor sugar
2 egg yolks
2 oz (50 g) raisins
Vanilla essence
Ground cinnamon
Brown sugar
Butter

Cut the croissants length ways and cut in half. Butter one side of the croissants and put to one side. Beat the egg yolks, caster sugar and milk, adding two drops of vanilla essence, then put aside. Grease an ovenproof dish and place a layer of croissants on the bottom, then sprinkle with raisins. Continue layering until all the croissants are used up.

Briefly beat the milk mixture, then pour over the croissants. Sprinkle with cinnamon. Leave to soak for at least 30 minutes.

Whilst the croissants are soaking, preheat the oven to Gas Mark 4 (180 °C, 350 °F).

Sprinkle a thin layer of brown sugar over the top of the dish then place in the middle of the oven for 20 minutes. Remove from the oven, add some more sugar and return to the oven for a further 20 minutes.

Baked Bananas

I have no doubt that if you have not tried this recipe, after tasting it you will be smitten. Make sure that you use dark chocolate as milk chocolate is just not the same.

Serves 4

Ingredients

**4 large bananas
4 oz (100 g) dark chocolate**

Pre-heat the oven to Gas Mark 6 (225 °C, 425 °F). Take a sharp knife and make an incision through the skin of the banana from end to end. Gently peel the skin apart and make another incision the length of the banana. Be careful not to pierce the other side of the skin. Break the chocolate into small pieces and then insert the chocolate in the cavity. Close the edges of the banana skin together, then wrap in tinfoil. Place the bananas in the oven for about 20 minutes or until they have softened and the chocolate has melted. Serve with thick double cream. These can also be cooked in the embers of a barbeque, where they will only take about 10 minutes.

Pancakes

Serves 4

Ingredients

4 oz (100 g) plain flour
1 egg
½ pint (300 ml) milk
A pinch of salt
Butter
Sugar
Lemon juice

Put the flour and salt in a bowl and add the egg into the middle. Pour in about a third of the milk. Stir gently, adding a little more milk in the process. Beat the mixture thoroughly, then add the rest of the milk. Stir well, then pour into a jug.

Melt a small piece of butter in a frying pan, then add a couple of tablespoons of the batter. Tip the frying pan to spread the mixture evenly. Fry until the underside is brown, then turn the pancake over with a fish slice or a knife and cook the other side.

Tip the finished pancake onto a plate and cover with lemon juice and sugar.

Biscuits and Cakes

The emphasis of this book is on preparing main meals rather than cakes and biscuits, as cooking main meals will be of more use. However, tea time comes round every afternoon, usually at about tea time, so an introduction to basic cake making is included.

Victoria Sponge

Two 7-inch (17 cm) sandwich tins are needed for this recipe.

Ingredients

6 oz (150 g) self-raising flour
6 oz (150 g) butter
4 oz (100 g) caster sugar
3 eggs, beaten
Jam

Mix together the sugar and butter until they are smooth in texture. Gradually add the eggs to the mixture, then fold in the flour. Grease the tins by wiping the inside of two 7-inch (17 cm) baking tins with a piece of greaseproof paper dabbed in butter. Divide the mixture between the two baking tins. Make sure that the tops of the cakes are level, then bake in the oven for 20 minutes or so at Gas Mark 5 (200 °C, 400 °F).

To see if a cake is cooked, stick a skewer in the centre of the sponge. If bits of the mixture are stuck to it when it is drawn out, it needs to be cooked a little longer. If the skewer comes out clean, the cake is ready.

Now turn the cakes out of the tins onto a wire rack (look in the grill pan for one). Once cooled, spread a layer of jam over one of the layers, sandwich the other one on top, and sprinkle with caster sugar.

Treacle Tart

This can be serve hot or cold, with cream or ice cream or on its own. Ideal as a snack or dessert.

Serves 4

Ingredients

4 oz (100 g) plain flour
2 oz (50 g) fresh white breadcrumbs
3 tbsp water
1 oz (25 g) lard
1 oz (25 g) butter
12 tbsp golden syrup
2 tsp grated lemon rind
Salt

Add a pinch of salt to the flour and sieve. Cut the fat into small pieces and rub them into the flour until the mixture resembles fine breadcrumbs. Add a tablespoon of water at a time until a firm dough is produced. Cover a clean surface or pastry board with a sprinkling of flour. Roll out the pastry so that there is enough to cover the bottom and the sides of an 8-inch (20 cm) flan dish. Mix the syrup, breadcrumbs and lemon juice together, then spoon into the flan case.

Bake for about 25 minutes at Gas Mark 6 (220 °C, 425 °F) until golden.

Chocolate Crunch

Ingredients

4 oz (100 g) digestive biscuits
4 oz (100 g) rich tea biscuits
4 oz (100 g) butter
3 oz (75 g) golden syrup
1 oz (25 g) cocoa powder
6 oz (150 g) plain chocolate
Icing sugar

Crush the biscuits by putting them in a clean bag, tying the ends of the bag and bashing with a rolling pin. Using a piece of grease-proof paper dabbed in butter, wipe the inside of a shallow baking tin. Melt the butter in a saucepan and add the syrup and cocoa, mix together then add the crushed biscuits. Remove from the heat. Stir the mixture thoroughly so that the biscuit crumbs are evenly coated. Transfer the biscuit mixture into the tin and press down the mixture using the back of a spoon and leave to cool.

To melt the chocolate place a Pyrex bowl on top of a pan of simmering water. Do not put too much water in the saucepan as there is a chance the water might boil over the edge. Place the chocolate in the bowl and let it melt. When the chocolate has completely melted remove the bowl from the heat using a pair of oven gloves and pour the chocolate over the biscuit mixture. Spread the chocolate so there is an even coating. Allow to cool, then cut into squares or slices. Dust with icing sugar.

Chocolate Cake

Ingredients

6 oz (150 g) self-raising flour
6 oz (150 g) butter
6 oz (150 g) caster sugar
3 eggs
1 ½ oz (40 g) cocoa
1 ½ tbsp water

For the icing:

8 oz (225 g) icing sugar
4 oz (100 g) plain cooking chocolate
1 ½ oz (40 g) butter or margarine
2 tbsp warm water

Place the sugar and the butter in a large mixing bowl and mix together, using either a wooden spoon or an electric mixer. Add the eggs, one at a time.

In a separate bowl, mix the flour and the cocoa powder together, then add it to the creamed mixture. Continue mixing, adding water until a soft dropping consistency is achieved.

Divide the mixture equally between two 7-inch (17 cm) sandwich tins. Bake in the oven at Gas Mark 5 (200 °C, 400 °F) for 25 to 30 minutes.

Test the cake with a skewer. If the mixture sticks to it, the cake needs a few more minutes in the oven.

When the cakes are ready, turn them out of their tins onto a wire rack.

Melt the chocolate by placing it in a basin and putting that over the top of a saucepan of boiling water. Be careful not to let the water boil over the top of the saucepan into the chocolate.

After the chocolate has melted, allow to cool. Cream together the butter and half the icing sugar, then add half the melted chocolate. Mix, and spread over one side of the cake, then 'sandwich' the two together.

The rest of the chocolate is used to make the icing on the top. Add the water and the rest of the sugar to the chocolate and spoon onto the top of the cake. Spread the icing around using a palette knife that has been dipped in hot water (this helps to spread the icing and stop it sticking to the knife).

The cake can be decorated with those little silver balls that break your teeth.

Flapjacks

Ingredients

8 oz (225 g) porridge oats
4 oz (100 g) butter
3 oz (75 g) sugar
4 tbsp golden syrup
A pinch of salt

Melt the butter in a large saucepan, then add the syrup and leave over a low heat for a couple of minutes. Remove from the heat and add the sugar, salt and oats. Mix thoroughly using a wooden spoon, making sure all the oats are covered with syrup.

Grease a shallow baking tray and evenly spoon in the mixture. Cook for 20 to 30 minutes at Gas Mark 4 (180 °C, 350 °F). After cooking, cut the flapjacks into bars before they cool.

Scones

A cream tea with thick scones oozing home-made jam and thick clotted cream tastes as good as anything found in a French patisserie.

Ingredients

8 oz (225 g) self-raising flour
2 oz (50 g) butter
¼ pint (150 ml) milk
A pinch of salt

Mix the flour and salt together. The flour is supposed to be sieved, but it's a bit time-consuming and doesn't make much difference anyway. Cut the margarine into small cubes and add them to the flour. Rub the mixture together using your fingers until the result looks like breadcrumbs.

Add the milk and stir in using the blade of a knife to form a soft dough. Roll out the mixture on a floured board until it is about half an inch (1.5 cm) thick. Cut into rounds using a biscuit cutter or a glass.

Grease a baking tray and place some scones on it, leaving enough gaps for them to rise. Brush some milk over the top of the scones to obtain a smooth and shiny finish.

Bake in a pre-heated oven for 10 to 15 minutes at Gas Mark 7 (230 °C, 450 °F).

Cheese Scones

As for plain scones, but stir in 4 oz (100 g) of cheese before adding the milk.

Fruit scones

As for plain scones, but stir in 1 oz (25 g) of sugar and 2 oz (50 g) of dried fruit before adding the milk.

Index

F

G

H